# Little Black Book of Comedy Sketches

Lance Tait

Theatre Metropole
Los Angeles, California

Copyright © 2007, 2012 by Lance Tait
Published by Theatre Metropole, Los Angeles.
All Rights Reserved.
No part of this book may be reproduced without the permission of the publisher. These plays are protected under Copyright Law. For permission to produce these works (worldwide), contact:
theatremetropole@yahoo.com

First Printing 2012

Publisher's Cataloging-In-Publication Data
(Prepared by The Donohue Group, Inc.)

Tait, Lance.
  Little black book of comedy sketches / Lance Tait.

  p. ; cm.

  Issued also as an ebook.
  ISBN-13: 978-1-4701-2922-4
  ISBN-10: 1-4701-2922-1

1. Comedy sketches. 2. American wit and humor. I. Title.

PS3570.A333 L58 2012
812/.54                                                      2012934320



ebook ISBN: 978-1-62154-256-8

Book design by Lise G. Neer
Cover design by Lise G. Neer

## Table of Contents

| | |
|---|---|
| Foreword | |
| The Over-Achiever | 7 |
| Mediocrity | 13 |
| Soap Opera | 19 |
| The Wild West | 24 |
| Sex in Advertising | 29 |
| The Talk T.V. Degenerate Syndrome | 35 |
| The Game of Life | 39 |
| Toothpick Monuments | 45 |
| At the Shrink's Office | 50 |
| Blast Off | 57 |
| After One Glass of Wine | 67 |
| Bats | 72 |
| Spaghetti | 76 |
| The Bee Farm | 80 |

# Foreword

I have selected fourteen out of the many comedy sketches that I wrote several years ago. Usually the sketches are for two actors: a female and a male; or two females, or two males. (In rare cases a sketch might have a third character.)

The average length of the sketches in this book is ten minutes. A theatrical show that brings together some six or seven of these sketches is probably just about right – if there is no intermission. Without an intermission, eight or more sketches in one night might try the patience of the best of audiences. It is suggested that group of four actors – two female, two male – might present such a show.

I hope readers and actors will find that the sketches I have chosen are funny. Audiences in Paris, and a couple of other testing grounds (New York and Los Angeles, each for one night) have.

The reason I wrote these sketches is because I encountered the fine French stage sketches of Roland Dubillard. The style of his sketches is unlike anything I've seen on North American or British television (I do not know the stage comedy sketch genre well.) I wanted to import the French style into English. (This is not to say however that I have been wholly uninfluenced by, say, the Marx Brothers.)

Dubillard was a poet/actor/playwright enjoyed by audiences – and esteemed by writers such as Samuel Beckett and Eugene Ionesco. Compared to the French models that inspired me, mine are coarser and perhaps less original. But with good acting, they can be funny.

Little or no character description, set description or stage directions are provided. To the actors who perform any of the skits in this book, please take special care with the pauses that separate blocks of dialog. These pauses indicate that something is going on: it can be characters' thoughts, their changes in position (blocking), a change of stage business – all motivated, of course, by the action of the sketch.

I caution actors not to believe that if you go faster, the audience will find you are funnier. If you proceed too quickly, those in the audience will likely miss something that is mentioned only once by a character; a member of the audience could lose important threads or strings in the slowly building ball of thread or string that finally gets big enough to make the sketch go over well with them. The characters in these sketches are often thinking – something often unexpected has been said to them. Give the characters time to think so that the audience members can also think – and laugh.

Also, actors, pay close attention to sound and rhythm. Meter, assonance, and alliteration are present in a great deal of poetry. They are present in these sketches. Exploit the patterns for comic effect.

With much gratitude I thank Ariane Dubillard, Gwylene Gallimard, so many friends, family members and actors.

Lance Tait

## 1. The Over-Achiever

*The action could take place indoors, somewhere outdoors, or in an abstract geometric space – the options are open.*

BABE: *(Female.)* So, what can I say but, Congratulations –
ABE: *(Male.)* Thanks.
BABE: You could say that with a little more feeling.
ABE: *(He is not joking.)* I said thanks. Thank you.
BABE: It's not everyone who wins a Nobel Prize. For MUSIC!
ABE: *(Also amazed at this.)* I know.
BABE: They created that prize this year only for you. It's never been done before. What a remarkable honor! You haven't made history, you ARE history.
ABE: Thank you.
BABE: You don't have to thank me for that. *(Pause.)* Somehow I feel this is all becoming so automatic for you.
ABE: What, I get something, and then I say, "Thank you"?

*Pride shows on* ABE's *face during the mention of his awards and accomplishments.*

BABE: You just don't get anything. Think of it, twelve years ago you received football's highest honor: Most Valuable Player... The next year you won an Oscar for Best Director.
ABE: All I did was write and produce a story about my mother.
BABE: Who was a coal miner's daughter and the first woman to walk on an asteroid.
ABE: Where funny enough, she found coal!
BABE: What an amazing movie.

• 7

ABE *has a dignified look about him as* BABE *continues.*

BABE: And... nine years ago you were elected president of the most powerful nation on earth. You served for eight years. During that time you halted global warming. You taught a billion people to love and respect the planet. You reversed the melting of the polar ice caps. Venice stopped sinking.
ABE: For that I got the key to the city.
BABE: Just think of the Pacific islanders who can now go back to their homes because they're not under water anymore.
ABE: I have the largest collection of hula skirts of any man in the world.
BABE: Do you always need to get a prize?
ABE: I don't set out to win them.

*Pride continues to show on* ABE'S *face.*

BABE: Don't tell me you didn't want the Conservative Club's Greatest Businessman Prize and the Liberal Club's Greatest Humanitarian Award.
ABE: They were feathers in my cap, I'll admit that.
BABE: But you don't seem that pleased. Have you ever been happy?
ABE: Always.
BABE: That's what you say. But I believe deep inside, you're suffering. You're troubled by... envy. *(Pause.)* You have nobody to be envious of! You yourself are an OBJECT of envy for others. Hey, when the United Nations recognizes you as a World Literary Treasure, you're going to have a few people who are jealous of you and your twenty novels.
ABE: They could have been jealous before when Japan declared me to be a National Treasure – and I'm not even Japanese.

*The Over-Achiever*

BABE: You're an honorary citizen.
ABE: Of that country and fifty others. It's good that I don't live in any of them. They'd be asking me to give them my time.
BABE: I know that's why you live in the mountains now. I still don't think you've made the adjustment there. You're not that comfortable living away from people.
ABE: I see people when I have to pick up my awards. But it's true, I do have to cope with specific problems... something motivates me, but also eats me... I became a medical doctor, a psychiatrist and a psychologist and I still can't get a grip on it.
BABE: "Know thyself."
ABE: Yeah, it's an important dictum.
BABE: But you're still a bit of a mystery to yourself.
ABE: At least I won the Mystery Writer of the Decade Prize given by the International Mystery Writers Society.
BABE: An organization highly respected even by the French – and you know they're picky.
ABE: Sometimes all these accomplishments are a little heavy.
BABE: Well, get a radio program and lighten up.
ABE: Everybody knows that a radio show takes up a lot of your time.
BABE: No, not with today's technology. You can do the show from your living room in seven minutes. Then technicians expand that to two hours. *(Pause.)* But you should just slow down. Writing a symphony a week, for example – that's a bit overboard. Ever since you got near an orchestra you've gone a little crazy.
ABE: The whole double-reed family of instruments fascinates me. *(Pause.)* Look, I don't manage boredom very well.

• 9

BABE: That's no excuse to allow yourself to be photographed around ten beautiful naked women – and have an eight page spread published worldwide.
ABE: It was public service advertisement for condoms to fight AIDS. The photographer was a friend of mine. I owed him a favor.
BABE: For what?
ABE: He reconnected me with my kids. It was so nice to be with my son and my daughter again. Children of divorce have such a tough time.
BABE: Children of high-achievers, too.
ABE: *(Reflecting.)* Part of it was their mother. She was Miss World and then she went to the Olympics and won gold medals in the high jump, in weightlifting and in skydiving.
BABE: It's not like you never won any gold medals there yourself – figure skating, the javelin, Acapulco cliff-diving...
ABE: Yeah, well.
BABE: You dismiss them because you moved on. Most people know you now for your spiritual depth.
ABE: Thanks. *(Pause.)* I'm not as deep as my ex-wife, though.
BABE: Which one?
ABE: The mother of my two children.
BABE: You're deep.
ABE: *(Pause. Unhappily.)* Didn't you hear the news?
BABE: What news?
ABE: She's been elected pope. The first woman ever intentionally made a Catholic pope.
BABE: You mean a woman's been elected a pope before, unintentionally?
ABE: Actually, yes. In the Middle Ages. They never looked up her robe. Now all the bishops have to get physicals. *(Pause.)* I knew it was going to happen. I knew she'd be Pope!

*The Over-Achiever*

BABE: Aren't you happy for her?
ABE: Well. *(Pause.)* You know, I started cooking last week.
BABE: Oh, yeah?
ABE: *(Very serious.)* Really cooking.
BABE: I suppose this means pretty soon you'll get an award for that.
ABE: If I ever do, it'll have to be given to me posthumously.
BABE: Posthumously?
ABE: Well, you see, soon I'll be cooking myself.
BABE: What?
ABE: They'll be small bits of me – that I've cut off and cooked.
BABE: I don't understand. *(Baffled, trying to come up with an answer.)* Is it for science?
ABE: I'm researching now. There's the question of sauces. I'm not convinced I taste all that great without them and I do want people to eat me.
BABE: Why?
ABE: Well, you remember, "Take this bread, it's my body – eat."
BABE: Yes. Jesus. *(Pause.)* You're not going the Jesus route?!

*Long pause.*

BABE: Does this have anything to do with your ex-wife being elected pope?
ABE: I'll show her I'm deeper!
BABE: You'll SHOW her? Obviously you're holding some kind of grudge.
ABE: I should never have married her. But we did have the kids, and that's a good thing. *(Pause. Stamps his foot on "not".)* I'm NOT going to let her get away with it!

BABE: Look what the world thinks of you! You're deep-deep. *(Pause.)* Let go! I know somebody like you can easily rise above... take the high road... You said you don't set out to win prizes.
ABE: I don't. But I have reasons.
BABE: Of course there's a reason behind each one of your achievements, but they're not so...

ABE *interrupts. He peers into the distance and speaks with great dignity:*

ABE: Purpose. Having something to live for.
BABE: But...

ABE *continues in his profound manner.*

ABE: When something motivates me, ...eats me, ...well, I have to act.
BABE: *(Pause.)* Have you ever thought about the concept of "going too far"?

ABE *blows up at* BABE.

ABE: You're driving me crazy, you know that!

ABE *then starts talking to himself.*

ABE: I'm not going to go insane! I'm not!

ABE *is having a crisis. A nervous tick shows. He spins back to* BABE *and yells.*

ABE: Stop!

## 2. Mediocrity

*The action most likely takes place near* BRAD's *cubicle, or, if he has one, his office.*

BRAD: I'm going to take myself out of the running for the job. You'd be a better manager than me.
ANNE: You're so selfless. I can't believe it.
BRAD: It's not that I'm selfless. I just doubt myself at this stage of my life.
ANNE: But you're very good.
BRAD: Not for that job.
ANNE: You'd be a good manager.
BRAD: Don't you want the job?
ANNE: Of course I do.
BRAD: Then you should be happy that I'm taking myself out of the running.
ANNE: I am in one sense – that is, for me. It makes it easier to tell you.
BRAD: What?
ANNE: Sorry to pull the genie out of the bag: they've already given ME the job.
BRAD: What! They gave YOU the job!
ANNE: Yes, me.
BRAD: But YOU!
ANNE: You don't think I'm qualified for it?
BRAD: Well, there are a lot of others...
ANNE: Like you. *(Pause.)* You said you didn't want it.
BRAD: No, I don't want it.
ANNE: *(Pause.)* Who do you think's more qualified than me?

BRAD *thinks. Pause. Then says:*

BRAD: No one. *(Pause.)* They made the right decision. You'll be great as a manager.
ANNE: Actually the job title is "Deputy Manager".
BRAD: Yeah, I know.
ANNE: *(Proudly.)* Deputy Manager of Mediocrity.
BRAD: Congratulations! Hang in there and they'll make you FULL manager when that position comes up. IF it ever comes up! Not too likely, huh? Morosco's got a lock on his job. *(Pause.)* Yeah, when he DIES, that'll change the situation.
ANNE: I wouldn't want him to die. I'm not that ambitious.
BRAD: That's just why they promoted you. You know, I bet you'll win the trophy for Deputy Manager of the Year.
ANNE: I'm not actually looking to win anything.
BRAD: The Department of Mediocrity has its rewards and you shouldn't shy away from them.
ANNE: No, but things happen just as often as a result of good intentions as they do from no intentions.

*Pause. He thinks.*

BRAD: That's true.
ANNE: *(Like she is quoting an adage.)* Just do your job, don't be too smart – or else you might be too smart for your own good.
BRAD: You put that thinking into action and for sure you'll win the Deputy Manager of the Year trophy!
ANNE: I don't care about trophies. But YOU seem to. Maybe you're frustrated.

*Pause.*

*Mediocrity*

BRAD: I'm thinking of putting in for a transfer.
ANNE: A transfer?
BRAD: Yeah, I haven't been the easiest guy to work with. Maybe the department's not the place for me. Maybe I'd be a lot happier in the Department of Hypocrisy.
ANNE: But they're such back-stabbers there.
BRAD: But I might thrive there.
ANNE: You're not a backstabber. Quite the opposite – look, you took yourself out of the running for Deputy Manager.
BRAD: It was only because it was in Mediocrity. *(Pause.)* I'm bored.
ANNE: Stay with mediocrity. It's for you.
BRAD: I know, but what can I do... I have this twinge ...it's hard to put my finger on it exactly because it's a psychological twinge. Have you ever had one of those?
ANNE: No.
BRAD: *(Almost to himself.)* Is it a challenge I need?...
ANNE: *(Firmly.)* You need to focus on something outside. Like... get into a new relationship with your television. Or shop for an exercise machine. Yeah, get distracted, now!
BRAD: I don't want a diversion. I want to BE one myself. I want to stand out from the crowd. I want to bring joy to people. I want to cause them problems.
ANNE: That's sounds DEVILISH...
BRAD: It IS sinister, isn't it?
ANNE: ...something the DEVIL might say.
BRAD: *(Pause. He clears his throat.)* Funny you should say, "Devil." I must say from time to time I find him interesting.

*Long pause.*

• 15

ANNE: So do I. *(Pause. Lowers her voice a little.)* Listen, I don't usually say anything, but, ah... *(Pause. Speaks in a possessed, disembodied voice.)* I belong to a congregation. We worship the Devil.

BRAD: That's exciting!

ANNE: It breaks the monotony of Mediocrity. Do you want to attend one of our services?

BRAD: Sure, why not? *(Pause. Amazed, surprised.)* I never pictured you...!

ANNE: We have a social hour after the service. Bring something for us to drink.

BRAD: *(Trying to be helpful.)* What?... rat's milk? Bat's blood?

ANNE: Coca-cola will be okay.

BRAD: You, a devil worshipper! Well, you never can tell! *(Pause.)* Wait a minute, does your being a devil worshipper have anything to do with you getting the promotion? Has your secret society infiltrated us?

ANNE: No. That kind of thing happens in Hypocrisy, not Mediocrity.

BRAD: *(Pause.)* Wow. *(Thinking.)* What do you do when you worship? Do you have orgies?

ANNE: I don't want to get your hopes up too high.

BRAD: Okay.

ANNE: But usually there's a lot of wild sex.

BRAD: Man! *(Pause.)* My life's taking a turn for the better.

ANNE: Or for the worse. It depends how you look at it.

BRAD: What do you mean?

ANNE: Well, at Devil worship, what most people call good, we call evil. We, like... INVERT things.

BRAD: That's understandable. This is such a change from the daily grind at the Department of Mediocrity!

ANNE: I don't know how I could survive in Mediocrity without my faith in the Devil. Without him, I'd feel just like you've been feeling – kind of down in the mouth.

*Pause.* BRAD *thinks a while, trying to take it all in.*

BRAD: Where do you and the others meet, anyway?
ANNE: When we're not outdoors we're in the usual places: churches, temples, mosques.
BRAD: Those places let you do what you do there?
ANNE: Sure. We only ever meet indoors on Thursdays. That's always downtime for them. We give them triple the asking price for rent. They're glad to take it.
BRAD: You're not really that mediocre, you know.
ANNE: It's good to become better friends with you. It's going to make my job as Deputy Manager so much easier.
BRAD: I know I haven't been the best co-worker lately. I've been irritable... But you will have no problems with me!

*Long pause.*

ANNE: I'm not really a Devil worshipper.
BRAD: What?
ANNE: No, I'm sorry. Just using a new management technique that I learned at a company-sponsored seminar this morning.
BRAD: What...? Really!? But wow! You're being way too creative for Mediocrity. What's happening?

ANNE: Well, you know the company has its low paid creative types that sometimes, once in a while, they listen to. It was decided that Mediocrity should use creative methods to get through to you and tell you that we value you as a mediocre person, we're used to you and we want you to fit in.
BRAD: So you used the Devil-worshipping trick to...
ANNE: *(Finishing his sentence.)* To bond with you. Listen, this is the best place in the world to work, don't you see? Snap out of it!
BRAD: There's always been a psychopathic element to Mediocrity.
ANNE: Oh, don't lash out at us. We like you.
BRAD: Isn't that nice.
Anne: Hey take the rest of the day off, go home and order a Chinese meal, sit back, relax, and think about this: nothing succeeds like mediocrity. Mediocrity's always in demand. We depend on it. Without it, life would cease to exist as we know it.

## 3. Soap Opera

*Someone whom the audience has not seen has just left.*

DON: *(Male.)* Who was that guy?
CHRIS: *(Female.)* Just somebody I know.
DON: Does he have a name?
CHRIS: Yeah.
DON: What is it?
CHRIS: Um... his name is Soap.
DON: *(Pause.)* That's a weird name.
CHRIS: Yeah, well, that's his name.
DON: Couldn't he stop so you could introduce us?
CHRIS: No, he had to go.
DON: He just slipped on by.
CHRIS: Yep.
DON: I guess that's why he's called "Soap".
CHRIS: Maybe.
DON: Not too polite, is he?
CHRIS: *(Defensively.)* He's got other things on his mind. *(Pause.)* I worry about him. His weight. He's got a weight problem.
DON: He looked okay to me.
CHRIS: He loses weight.
DON: *(Venturing a guess.)* Has he been... wasting away?
CHRIS: Sort of. It's not a complete... waste. He does get things done – he cleans things. But...
DON: But in the process he loses something.
CHRIS: Yeah. Soap could shrink to nothing if he's not careful.
DON: Maybe Soap should change his name.
CHRIS: What good would that do?
DON: He should change his name to "Dirt".

CHRIS: What?! Nobody's going to like somebody called "Dirt."
DON: This is what could happen: Soap changes his name to Dirt. Then he works to give dirt a better reputation.
CHRIS: Why would he want to do that?
DON: *(Explaining.)* For some reason I sense that Soap might be just the type of guy who wants to do good in the world – whatever people wind up calling him.
CHRIS: I don't how you can think that. Actually, you don't know him. You saw him for like... three seconds.
DON: That was enough. And with a name like that...
CHRIS: Maybe he wouldn't do good if he changed his name.
DON: Yeah, you're right, who knows? *(Pause.)* There's a big fork in the road for us.
CHRIS: What?
DON: *(By "place" he means her house or apartment.)* Your place is filthy.
CHRIS: Oh, this is what this has all been working up to. *(Defensively.)* I clean my silverware when it's dirty.
DON: I don't mean fork in that sense.
CHRIS: Why are you bringing fork in the ROAD to it? There's no road here.
DON: I know why Soap left without saying anything to me. It was because you told him to behave like that. *(Pause.)* Look, I'm going to go out on a limb and say you're PROTECTING Soap. *(Pause. Protesting.)* You're afraid of something that you don't need to be afraid of! Soap can always be around. Don't think you're preserving Soap's life. What you're doing is endangering the wellbeing of another person – in this case, ME.
CHRIS: What?

*Soap Opera*

DON: The way you keep your place – I get sick when I come over. All because of your concern for Soap and his quote, "weight problem".
CHRIS: He's really a nice guy.
DON: So *I* don't matter? *(Pause.)* I have allergies. Dirt should be kept at a reasonable minimum.
CHRIS: Leave dirt out of this!
DON: Okay, so if you want to save Soap a little bit, get out a bucket of water and a sponge sometimes. Just with water.
CHRIS: I wash.
DON: Very little. Look, we all have our peculiarities. Your friendship with Soap does in a way contradict itself. You care about him, yet you push him away. Why?
CHRIS: *(A stark admission.)* It's true that I don't personally see a lot of Soap.
DON: You have a Savior Complex. Only he can save himself. Only he can re-invent himself and solve his weight problem – if that's what needs to be done. *(A pause.)* If you really cared about other human beings, you wouldn't be afraid of USING Soap. People use other people like they use soap. It cleanses them. There's nothing wrong with it, in fact, it's right.
CHRIS: I wash clothes and dishes!
DON: Do you USE Soap?
CHRIS: That's none of your business.
DON: See, that pushes me away from you. You push people away from you. You leave them in the dust.
CHRIS: *(Flustered, worried.)* You...you say there's a BIG FORK. Let me pick it up.
DON: You can't pick it up. It's not on the floor. It's there. *(Pointing into the atmosphere.)* It's THE PROBLEM. It won't go away.

• 21

CHRIS: What if I fill up the sink with water and call Soap to come over?
DON: It's too late. I'm grossed out. I've been sick. It's traumatized me.
CHRIS: We can start again!
DON: *(Pause.)* Look, Chris, I can't be with you anymore. You live like a pig.
CHRIS: Study any book about animals and they'll tell you that, in fact, pigs are very clean animals.
DON: I apologize to the pigs.
CHRIS: Well, you should apologize to me.
DON: You have too many excuses. I can't apologize to you.
CHRIS: Oh, this is so sad.
DON: Life can be sad.
CHRIS: Life shouldn't be like that. It doesn't have to be.
DON: That's what you say, but what are you DOING? The condition of your apartment demonstrates your lack of concern for me and the rest of the people who...
CHRIS: I don't want to be sad!
DON: My only advice is to change your relationship with Soap – actually, going it alone with water certainly will never be enough. *(Pause.)* I have to go.
CHRIS: But if I change, will you come back?
DON: No, I've had enough. Things are soiled between us.
CHRIS: *(Pause. Starts to cry.)* Look, I'm crying. *(Pause.)* Our problems have turned into some kind of soap opera.
DON: I think it's different than that.
CHRIS: What do you mean?
DON: In soap operas they never actually have a problem with Soap.

*Soap Opera*

CHRIS: *(Weeping.)* But the commercials!
DON: This isn't a commercial. *(Pause.)* I'm sorry things are way they are. What can I say? You're stuck in a rut. It doesn't look like you'll change. I'm not the least bit sexually interested in you anymore. Some people are filthy sluts. You're not a slut. You're just ... filthy.
CHRIS: *(Still weeping, blurts out:)* At least I'm not a slut.
DON: At least you're not a slut. Well, goodbye.
CHRIS: No, don't go!
DON: It's that fork in the road.
CHRIS: Let's go out to dinner and talk about it. There's a favorite place of mine. We'll use chopsticks!
DON: No. You need to get Soap back first. Not me. I know it's going to be hard. But start by thinking "Hygiene." Bye.

DON *leaves.*

CHRIS: *(Crying, then settling down, talking herself through the problem.)* One door closes, another opens. Something good always comes from misfortune. Nobody cares about Soap the way I do. A mess has meaning. The world's a mess! *(Pause.)* Why do I always pick neat-freaks to go out with!?!

# 4. The Wild West

*Two cowboys wear cowboy hats. The year is approximately 1860.*

ABNER: Jeez, oh, boy, if the Wild West didn't exist, somebody'd have to invent it!
BUZZ: It's a real cornucopia, I'll give you that. Red skins thumping drums, white women smoking cigars, negroes with sneaky habits... Fortune hunters, buffalo skinners, sodomists!
ABNER: Banks aching to be held up. Whores buyin' whips and chains. New, strange birds wanting to be painted by scientists who also are digging up weird skeletons of dragons or something like it.
BUZZ: Lynchin's, drinkin'.
ABNER: More lynchin's and exterminations of whole tribes! Pledges of abstinence!
BUZZ: The Wild West is full of action.
ABNER: It's really a great big mess, if you ask me. Anarchy. So little government that it's the thugs that rule.
BUZZ: Organized government ain't the answer.

*Pause.*

BUZZ: You know that new guy in town, Abdul?
ABNER: I know Abdul. Only drinks sassafras.
BUZZ: He's the one. He says there's always going be bullies. Says there's a correct alternative to it all. He says we don't have to live like we live.

*The Wild West*

ABNER: Yeah, well he doesn't drink beer or whiskey.
BUZZ: He says it goes farther than that. *(Pause.)* You know, he's learnin' me how to read.
ABNER: Readin's a little hard for me.
BUZZ: If you want, I betcha he can learn you how to read, too.
ABNER: Oh, I don't know if I got the patience for it.
BUZZ *holds up sign which says,* "FOUR YEARS LATER".

ABNER *sings roughly, to the tune of "Twinkle, Twinkle, Little Star:"*

ABNER: "A-B-C-D-E-F-G, that's what Allah gives to me."
BUZZ: Yeah, he given us a real education, ain't he?
ABNER: And a lot more.
BUZZ: He gives us calmness of the heart. It's been so fast the way that old Islam has caught on in the Wild West. I tell you that Abdul had more voyages than Sinbad!
ABNER: I cannot only read English, I can read Ay-ray-bic!
BUZZ: Me, too. I'm so glad he came to the United States. and he survived all the petty name calling and death threats that people done to him. America is such a land of opportunity.
ABNER: *(Taking a piece of paper out of his pocket.)* Hey, look at this. Somebody give it to me for a Ramadan present.
BUZZ: What is it?
ABNER: It's an old place mat. And on it been drawn all the pilgrimage sites that you can visit in Mecca.
BUZZ: That's really fine. *(Looks closely at it.)* I recognize that.
ABNER: Yeah, I'm saving up my money hard to get to Mecca. Who would've thought that I'd be converted to Islam when I was brought up a Baptist?
BUZZ: Me too. I guess our upbringing made it natural for us to just to segue right into the prophet Mohammad's camp.

• 25

ABNER: Yeah, it feels so right, don't it? (*Pause.*) I never would have thought I had been born an infantile.
BUZZ: You mean infidel. (*Pause.*) But all is forgiven when you get with the One and Only God. (*Longer pause.*) Hmm, the way I see it, our country's gonna have harmonious relations with all the lands of the world from here on out. From here to Europe to China there's Mohammedans spread everywhere.
ABNER: Too bad Abdul won't be around no longer to see the progress our country's making.
BUZZ: Yep, too bad.
ABNER: Ever since he exploded under spontaneous circumstances there's been a big hole in town.
BUZZ: That's because he blowed up Downtown. If it had been on the outskirts, it would've been a smaller hole.
ABNER: I am so happy to hear they're putting a plaque on the mosque to honor him.
BUZZ: Well, we got Akbar around now to minister to the masses. But I don't like the way he dresses.
ABNER: He don't dress to fit in, does he?
BUZZ: That's coz he's what you call orthodox.
ABNER: I thought orthodox is who you go to when you got something wrong with your teeth.
BUZZ: No, that's a dentist.

*Pause.*

ABNER: I got to say. Sometimes I have my doubts.
BUZZ: (*Suspicious.*) About what?

*The Wild West*

ABNER: No, it's nothing like that. I still say my prayers five times a day facing east. I have my doubts that I'll ever get to Mecca. It's so far away. I have a hard enough time getting out of town to go huntin'.
BUZZ: But you know the learnin's: you can still go to heaven even if you don't make it to Mecca 'least one time in your life. What counts is that you got to TRY to get to Mecca.
ABNER: Well, yeah, I'm saving up. But at the rate I've saving, I ain't getting to Mecca for another three hundred and twenty-five years.
BUZZ: Listen, there's another way of getting to Mecca.
ABNER: No, I ain't gonna steal from nobody. Stealing is bad. I'll get my hand cut off for it. Both hands maybe!
BUZZ: I'm talking about another way of trying.
ABNER: No, I ain't gonna hijack a boat. If I get caught, then they'll cut off my... I don't what they'd cut off! What WOULD they cut off?

*Pause.* BUTCH *takes something out of his pocket and shows it to* ABNER.

BUZZ: Look here.
ABNER: What do you got there?
BUZZ: It's something they call hashish.
ABNER: You don't say. What you showing me that for?
BUZZ: It's the only way some people can afford to get to Mecca.
ABNER: What, you sell it to get there?
BUZZ: No, you smoke it.
ABNER: And then what happens?
BUZZ: You know the story about the magic carpet that flies?
ABNER: I do.

Buzz: You smoke some of this here hashish and a carpet comes and whisks you off to Mecca.
Abner: Golly. Did I miss something about this in the Koran?
Buzz: This ain't mentioned there. But it's entirely legal.
Abner: Islamic culture is so advanced! *(Pause.)* I have been so worried about getting to Mexico before I die.
Buzz: You mean, Mecca.
Abner: Didn't I say that?
Buzz: You did. *(Pause.)* Why don't we just go off and smoke some of this right now? No point in you being anxious.
Abner: Wow, I can't believe it! I'm going get to Mecca a lot sooner than I ever thought. Allah is great!
Buzz: You bet he is. And this hashish costs you only five cents.
Abner: Boy, it's so economical.
Buzz: That's because it's the will of Allah. Allah's very interested in economy. You wait, something's going happen. He's going do something really fabulous for THE economy... like, you know them new-fangled railroads they got? Well, one day, trains are gonna run on a fuel that right now you can only dream about when you smoke hashish. And that fuel,... let's call it... SLIME... is going be in all the important places... places where the Islamic folks live, like here in Texas and over there in Arabia.
Abner: I don't exactly understand what you say. You've always been a tad ahead of me. Can't say I hold it 'gainst you since you always seem to steer me right.
Buzz: Well, come on then, let's go on over by the corral and smoke up. Then I'll take you 'round to some of Mecca's shrines.

*They exit.*

## 5. Sex in Advertising

*The action could take place in an office at an advertising agency or it could take place afterhours in a quiet room in a house where a party is going on. These are only suggestions.*

ALAN: *(Offstage.)* Sex is important in advertising. As important as it is in real life.

ALAN *and* BRANDI *enter.*

BRANDI: Sex isn't all that it's cracked up to be.
ALAN: Yeah?
BRANDI: It's really rather disgusting when you think about it.
ALAN: It could be that you're just perverted.
BRANDI: Maybe people that value sex are perverted.
ALAN: You've obviously got a problem with sex.
BRANDI: *(For human society, in general:)* Sex IS a problem. It's not my problem, though.
ALAN: Well, you seem to have a problem with it.
BRANDI: No. But if you think about it, sex is pretty disgusting, isn't it?
I think that vomit's disgusting but I recognize it happens from time to time and that it smells bad and it's sickening to look at. That's because the body's been interrupted in its normal digestive process and then you see the process revealed – you're not supposed to see it – it looks awful.
ALAN: So you're not supposed to see sex. When you see it, it looks awful.

BRANDI: Who said that? Why are you comparing sex to vomiting?
ALAN: I wasn't, you were.
BRANDI: No, I wasn't. But I don't want to talk about sex. I was only making a remark after you said that sex is important in advertising – as important as it is in real life. I shouldn't have said anything.
ALAN: You don't deny that sex is important in advertising.
BRANDI: Yes, sex draws people.
ALAN: But it's disgusting when you think about it.
BRANDI: Actually you FEEL it more than you think it. *(Pause.)* You might agree with me... *(Pauses to think, then:)* When was the last time you had sex?
ALAN: It's been quite a while. How about you?
BRANDI: *(With the tone of, "How dare you!")* Why do you ask me that?
ALAN: You probably don't bother to have sex.
BRANDI: How do you know?
ALAN: It disgusts you.
BRANDI: Yeah, so?
ALAN: You're not saying you've had sex recently.
BRANDI: Well...
ALAN: How recently?
BRANDI: Five hours ago.
ALAN: You're lying.
BRANDI: No, it's true.
ALAN: Why did you do it if you find it disgusting?
BRANDI: I made a mistake. Maybe I convinced myself I was just doing research.
ALAN: So it was a mistake to have sex?

*Sex in Advertising*

BRANDI: Don't envy me.
ALAN: Well...
BRANDI: If you were me, you'd find sex revolting.
ALAN: I want to have had sex five hours ago.
BRANDI: What good would that do you now?
ALAN: At least the glow of it would still be with me.
BRANDI: That's disgusting – the glow.
ALAN: Somehow I'm not surprised to hear you say that.
BRANDI: Sex is only good when you're having it. After that, it's nauseating.
ALAN: I'm interested... just how long AFTER sex do you find the whole thing disgusting?
BRANDI: About thirty seconds.
ALAN: That's not long. So the glow only lasts that long.
BRANDI: I don't have a sensation of glow.
ALAN: You do have a problem with sex.
BRANDI: I do my best to not make it my problem. Sometimes I fail. I feel dirty. I feel it's been a waste of time.
ALAN: A waste of your time. What about the other person? I bet they don't think they're wasting their time.
BRANDI: I don't care what my partner thinks. As far as I'm concerned, I think they're in the same trap as I am: The Body and Its Passions.
ALAN: Maybe you're in a relationship with the wrong person.
BRANDI: No, I find all sex pretty nauseating.
ALAN: Too bad for you.
BRANDI: It's all vastly, vastly overrated.
ALAN: You're only dismissing sex because you've had it recently. If you hadn't had it, you'd be like me, craving it.

• 31

BRANDI: I did crave it. It was horrible.
ALAN: Now it's still horrible for you.
BRANDI: It's a universal trap.
ALAN: So allow that trap to come between you and business. We have to sell. And sex sells. That's why next to the product we're selling there's a sexy woman, or something like that.
BRANDI: I don't have anything against that. *(Pause.)* The product's important. After all, it's what ultimately pays my mortgage.
ALAN: So in one sense, sex doesn't disgust you. *(Pause.)* I'm not like you. Most people aren't like you.

BRANDI *switches off and is thinking in her own space.*

ALAN: *(Pause.)* I've got it! You should kill yourself. You're unhappy, you don't like real sex. But you do have a relationship with the stimuli that arouse everybody else.

*Pause. A series of extraordinary insights hits* BRANDI:

BRANDI: Sex is wet. Advertising is dry. Advertising will always be dry. Things that we're selling have the potential to be wet... – but no, no, ads will always be dry. And I like dry. I don't like wet! *(This is spoken like a revelation:)* It's the wetness that's disgusting!
ALAN: That's why you don't like working on the adult diaper account!
BRANDI: Yes! Yes!
ALAN: You can only tolerate a certain amount of wetness. A little bit – maybe thirty seconds' worth –

BRANDI: Yes, yes! I want it dry!
ALAN: And clean?
BRANDI: Yes!
ALAN: Do you believe in God, a God that is, for all intents and purposes, male, solar, that is, not feminine, earthy –
BRANDI: I never thought about it, but yes, I do!
ALAN: ...a man-god in pressed, clean diapers that are never soiled, a universe where you don't see vomit –
BRANDI: Yes, yes.
ALAN: *(To self.)* I think I'm describing Heaven. *(To* BRANDI:*)* ...Sex that's dry?
BRANDI: Yes, yes, if only it could be that way!
ALAN: But it is that way. We're in advertising! *(Thinks. A pause.)* I was wrong to say you should kill yourself. If advertising didn't exist, then I'd say, go ahead, shoot yourself! But God appears to you through advertising!
BRANDI: You're right! *(Pause.)* Wait. *(Pause.)* I'm having a flash!

*Pause.*

BRANDI: "The extraordinary... the secret...
the secret beginning...
the secret continues...
your tongue is a sensitive organ.
now taste the supreme... pleasure.
ONE DREAM CHOCOLATE...
sends shivers up...
smooth but hard...

BRANDI *lowers herself to gently towards the floor, and looks up at the ceiling. A pause.*

BRANDI: And then we see a beautiful woman in the spring rain and her clothes are wet! Wet enough to see that she's VERY satisfied. ...Oh, God!

*She lets out an orgasmic cry. Then she collects herself. She starts to get up.*

BRANDI: *(Cooling off a bit.)* Well, it's just a start.
ALAN: Let me help you. *(Pause. He helps her up from the floor.)* Wow, now I know why you're one of the stars of this business!

# 6. The Talk T.V. Degenerate Syndrome

*The action most likely takes place in* BURT's *office.*

ALISON: I got up this morning, looked in the mirror and I didn't see a thing! There was no reflection.
BURT: Oh, no –
ALISON: I can't tell my producer. (*Pause.*) He'd think I'm weird. Then he might tell somebody at the network. Somebody on the board might hear about it. If they don't really like me, they could use it to get back at me. They'll suggest I be replaced. Even though my ratings are high. (*Pause.*) I tried other mirrors in the house. The same thing: no reflection. What's going on?
BURT: I've seen it before.
ALISON: You have?
BURT: You've got the Talk T.V. Degenerate Syndrome.
ALISON: What's that?
BURT: You're on the air everyday. You always have an answer for anybody's question. You always have an answer even when there's no question.
ALISON: And I've got a statement to make when others are speechless. People tune in because they can count on me to say what's what.
BURT: You're paid to keep talking.
ALISON: It's not as basic as that. I have skills. Knowledge.
BURT: It's not natural to talk so much. That's what causes the degeneration. Do you mind not seeing your reflection?

ALISON: What if my hair's a mess and I don't know that it needs combing because I can't see myself? And then I go out into public and people laugh at me?
BURT: That's a serious problem. *(Pause.)* So you'd like to be able to see your reflection in a mirror?
ALISON: *(Impatient and angry.)* Yes!
BURT: The only known cure is to stop appearing on television. And no talking in public – even if there are no cameras. *(Pause.)* Slowly your reflection'll come back to you.
ALISON: *(Protesting.)* I don't have time for that!
BURT: It's the only way.
ALISON: I have my show and I make a lot of money.
BURT: What's more important, the money or your health?
ALISON: How do you know so much about the Talk T.V. Degenerate Syndrome?
BURT: You know I used to have a job like yours. Then one day I looked in the mirror and I had the same problem you do. I was lucky to run into somebody that same week whose opinion I highly respect. She told me that she thought I was a degenerate.
ALISON: That was just her opinion.
BURT: *(Finishing his thought.)* So I connected the dots between her opinion of me and what had happened to my reflection.
ALISON: You connected the dots?

*The Talk T.V. Degenerate Syndrome*

BURT: You could say I reflected. I realized that what had happened to me was a natural reaction to an unnatural action. Each of us has only so much to say. And if we keep talking without thinking, then we're not really saying anything. If we keep on talking despite the fact that we have nothing to say sooner or later nature will call our bluff. *(Pause.)* You think it's a bad thing that you can't see anybody when you look in the mirror. But the joke's on you! Because in all probability, it's been weeks, maybe even months, since a lot of people have noticed that the human you has checked out of your body. *(Pause.)* I'm sure you've gotten letters, emails from people who've called you a degenerate. Maybe even a few guests on the air have tried to call you that! Well, there's something in what people say – even though they don't know that "degenerate" can actually be a medical condition. You didn't pay attention to those people and their comments. You said they were wackos.
ALISON: I'll learn to live without mirrors. I want to work.
BURT: But what about your hair, what if you're seen in public...
ALISON: *(Interrupting.)* From now on I'll have a personal assistant with me at all times.
BURT: Is it worth that much to you to stay on the air?
ALISON: You don't know me. There are some sacrifices you need to make to stay on top.
BURT: To stay on top of what?

• 37

ALISON: Listen, I'm not going to start thinking about what it is that I'm on top of. I just know I'm on top. That works for me. Let people call me a degenerate. Let them talk all they want. Hey, I talk all I want, so why can't they! The only difference is that I'm the one with the television show, and I can pull the plug on them whenever I want to, and I do!
BURT: Okay, well. *(Pause.)* I wouldn't worry about your producer's reaction to all this. He's got enough problems of his own.
ALISON: Yeah, like what?
BURT: For starters, ...haven't you ever noticed? He doesn't have a shadow.
ALISON: What's that mean?
BURT: You'll figure it out.
ALISON: *(Changing the subject.)* I have to get ready for my interview with the governor. Boy, is SHE a degenerate!
BURT: She has her problems.
ALISON: *(Dismissively.)* Everybody does.
BURT: You have no idea. I'd be more careful about using the word "degenerate". It could actually mean something.
ALISON: By the time I get through with it, it won't mean a thing!

## 7. The Game of Life

*A television game show is in progress.*

HOST: *(Male.)* Before we ask you the big question we like to let those viewers that just tuned in know something about you.
CONTESTANT: *(Female. Enthusiastically:)* Big question? I'll say it's a big question!
HOST: If you answer the question correctly then you'll win ONE MILLION DOLLARS! That's not small change!
CONTESTANT: Nobody said it was.
HOST: So. *(Reads from a card in his hand.)* You are Chris Martin and you live in Probabliopolis, East Virginolino.
CONTESTANT: That's correct.
HOST: You work in reinsurance, which is something like insurance on insurance.
CONTESTANT: Yes. *(Pause.)* I'm so excited.
HOST: I'm sure nothing as exciting as this has ever happened to you before.
CONTESTANT: The only thing that comes close is when I was dating two men at the same time and one gave me a diamond necklace and the other, a car.
HOST: *(Thinking, "You manipulative slut.":)* Not bad. *(Looking at his card.)* I see here you're a Scorpio, a biter – but gentle when you caress. *(Chuckling.)* Scorpio – like that means anything! Ha! Astrology! But you women go for it! *(Pause.)* We aim to please ...whatever! Chris, how does being a Scorpio actually impact your life? *(Pause. Warning her pleasantly.)* Don't lie...
– Ha! *(Hurrying:)* That's not the big question, don't answer it. It's enough for us to know that like many people you COMMUTE TO WORK! *(Pause. A change of tone.)*

• 39

Host: *(Continued.)* You, Chris Martin, could become an instant millionaire if you answer the next question correctly. Are you ready?
Contestant: I'm ready.
Host: If you're wrong, that's it, you know.
Contestant: I can't think of that now.
Host: *(Expansively.)* You've been with us through so many questions. You've triumphed over the others. If you hadn't, you wouldn't be here now!
Contestant: I know.
Host: *(Expansively.)* We've asked you questions about entertainment, about geography, celebrity history, deviants and post-partum depression! We've caught you off guard – seen you at your worst! When you've tried to hide your disappointment over not being able to identify the Black Sea coast town of Sebastopol, we've felt for you. Then we've seen you rally. We've seen you get angry as we inadvertently uncovered ONE of your parents' unsuccessful battles with alcoholism. Are you ready?
Contestant: I said I was. *(Pause.)* I'm so exited I have to pee.
Host: You can't do that, we're on national T.V. But you're really ready, besides that, right?
Contestant: I'm ready.
Host: Are you really, really ready?
Contestant: Dammit, I'm ready.
Host: We'll fix that swear word. In fact, the engineers'll probably take the whole sentence out. People never know how much cursing goes on these shows.
Contestant: Why are you slowing me down, just ask the fucking question!

*The Game of Life*

HOST: *(Snaps at her.)* We're building suspense. *(Pause.)* Okay. For ONE MILLION DOLLARS, who was the first president of the United States?
CONTESTANT: Wait. That's too simple. It's a trick question. *(Pause.)* And when's the last time somebody actually won a million dollars on this program? You guys always find a way to squirm out of it. *(Pause.)* There's no way the answer to that question is what I think it is. Let me think. The question is...
HOST: Who was the first president of the United States of America?
CONTESTANT: All right. So we have, the United States of America. 1776, Declaration of Independence. The war with Britain. George Washington is a general and fights in the war. You don't need to know that. You only need to know who the first president is. Why would you hand me a million on a silver platter? Because you aren't! You never pay out. You're cheapskates!
HOST: *(Taunting her.)* Sometimes you have to EARN your money.
CONTESTANT: Yep, you always think of a way to get out of it. That's why your show is called, "Life". You build me up, and then let me down. You've done it to all the contestants. Why'd I get involved in this? I had no choice. I didn't ask to be born.
HOST: Please answer the question.
CONTESTANT: You're worse than pus that a cockroach finds and feeds to its young.
HOST: We're not talking about insects, we're talking about presidents.

CONTESTANT: I know it's not George Washington. It can't be. You and your staff are the lowest. All you want to do is use and humiliate people. And you think it's entertainment.
HOST: You have five seconds to answer the question.
CONTESTANT: *(Pause.)* The answer is... *(She gestures obscenely as she says:)* Up Yours, Buddy!
HOST: "Up Yours, Buddy" is not the answer. You lose. The correct answer is George Washington.
CONTESTANT: Wait... wait... I've got it. The correct answer... is... John Hanson. He was president between 1776 and 1778 and then, there were seven more presidents before Washington – who only became president in 1794.
HOST: You're wrong. It was George Washington.
CONTESTANT: I know you people. If I'd said Washington, you would have said it was incorrect – the right answer was John Hanson.
HOST: But YOU never said either one of those names.
CONTESTANT: That's because I'm not going let myself to be humiliated!

*Program music starts.*

HOST: Thanks for being a contestant on "Life". We're sending you home with a BRAND NEW REFRIGERATOR-FREEZER!
CONTESTANT: You can shove that where the sun don't shine! *(Pause. Practically in tears.)* Can't I get a break!? Why is everything a struggle? Sure I had my two boyfriends, both at the same time – am I being punished for that? I may be a Scorpio, but I have a brain. And I think. I actually USE my brain.

*The Game of Life*

Host: We're so happy you do. Now, just shuffle off the stage.
Contestant: This is what you give me for all my effort?
Host: *(Announcing to the audience.)* A BRAND NEW REFRIGERATOR-FREEZER!
Contestant: I was happy to get on the show. It's not easy. Some many people try. They're rejected. All I got was a higher level of rejection.
Host: *(To the audience.)* That's our show for tonight. *(To her:)* Better luck next time!
Contestant: You know as well as I do there's no next time.
Host: *(To her only:)* There's always heaven. *(To the audience:)* Thanks for tuning in! See you next time!
Contestant: I didn't tell you this before. I've got four pounds of explosives taped to my body. I can blow this whole place up!
Host: That's against the rules. And if you do it, we'll be off the air anyway.
Contestant: *(Weeping.)* This is the final... go 'round for me. Everything I've tried has failed. Everything I've done in good faith and sincerity... has been answered by... disappointment. I don't want to blow anybody up. I'm a thinking, feeling, respectful person, not a terrorist. I want to live, to live. I just want to be put to work using my skills. I want to be... happy! Why is that such an impossible thing?

*The following is said to the studio audience, but the* HOST *knows it will be edited out.*

HOST: What a load of crap! Security! Take her away. How'd she get let on the program? *(Pause.)* People. You'd think they'd be satisfied with their fifteen minutes of fame – but no, it's not enough! *(Pause.)* I've got a wife and two kids. I can't risk a thing! Everything I say is completely scripted. At least you get a chance to be YOU. I'VE never been a contestant. I never get a chance to show off how much I know. You don't know how lucky you are to have the freedom to say in public that you're disappointed!

*The* HOST *says the following, knowing that it won't be edited out. He's upbeat:*

HOST: That's life for now!

## 8. Toothpick Monuments

*In a general store in a small town in America. The year is 1919.* ALVIN *is a young man on wooden crutches.* BILLIE, *female, much older, works in the store.*

ALVIN: I've learned so much about design. The architecture! What an eye-opener. Italy, Spain, France, Switzerland, Germany, Austria – they have a feeling... they have taste. Now I'm ready to begin building the monuments I've wanted to build.
BILLIE: Who's going to sponsor you?
ALVIN: I don't need a sponsor that gives me money, if that's what you mean. *(Pause.)* Moral support would always be welcome.
BILLIE: You can count on me for that. *(Pause.)* So how are you getting the money to build your monuments?
ALVIN: Myself.
BILLIE: You're not rich.
ALVIN: I don't need to be.
BILLIE: But you envision... what... fifteen monuments?
ALVIN: Something like that.
BILLIE: But how are you going to fund them?
ALVIN: They're not going to be expensive.
BILLIE: No? *(Pause.)* Concrete isn't expensive... but still, it'll add up.
ALVIN: Nothing will be made out concrete.
BILLIE: You're using stone?
ALVIN: I'll be using toothpicks.
BILLIE: What?

• 45

ALVIN: And they don't cost a lot.
BILLIE: You said you learned so much studying the architecture you saw in Europe.
ALVIN: That's just it. I've learned to fit the design to the subject. After a lot of thought, I've settled on toothpicks.
BILLIE: You're not just trying to save money?
ALVIN: Not at all. They'll be perfect.
BILLIE: They'll be out of wood. And they'll be small.
ALVIN: Tiny.
BILLIE: Nobody will see them if they're that size.
ALVIN: Everybody will see them if they're small. *(Pause.)* A subject has to earn its space. It shouldn't take up space just for the sake of taking it up.
BILLIE: People associate monuments with bigness.
ALVIN: I have to remain true to my principles. To what I think. For example, I think human civilization is on its way down. And I'm building monuments for the beings that come after. They'll be more likely to find my monuments, tucked away somewhere, maybe in a grave or a cave that hasn't been blown up or melted or whatever. Like you know what anthropologists find today, art and artifacts of ancient cultures – well, they'll find ours, in the future. *(Pause.)* Things like pyramids grab the headlines but it's the little trinkets that really stand as true monuments to a culture.
BILLIE: So you're going to build trinkets.
ALVIN: No, true monuments.
BILLIE: People will think they're models.
ALVIN: People as we know them are not going to exist.
BILLIE: So you've got a long-range view of things.

*Toothpick Monuments*

ALVIN: Isn't that what a monument is about? *(Pause.)* People have such an inflated view of just who we are. They should see my monuments – that will make them think.
BILLIE: When people see your monuments, they'll say you're being negative. A politician would say you're being unpatriotic.
ALVIN: One of the smallest monuments I plan to build is one dedicated to politicians.
BILLIE: So I guess you're not concerned about criticism of your project by people that are living today.
ALVIN: My monuments are commemorative of what I've witnessed and what's touched me deeply.
BILLIE: I don't think toothpicks are going to work. *(Pause.)* I have to say it... you're a depressive type.
ALVIN: You're wrong there. I may be melancholy – that's different.
BILLIE: What's the difference?
ALVIN: Depressed people are less likely to build monuments. They can't act. They mope. Whereas melancholy people...
BILLIE: Are more likely to build monuments.
ALVIN: Not necessarily. But they do have hard to express feelings about what the world will be like in a million years. *(Pause.)* And if and when they build something, they make a Testament *(Pause.)* You see, that's what I'm doing. *(Pause. Expansively.)* For a monument builder, it's the ART of testament.
BILLIE: I never liked modern art much.
ALVIN: *(He looks into the distance.)* So much is in the dark. That's what happens when the world starts winding down.
BILLIE: You're gloomy. The world's got problems, but...

ALVIN: And a lot's in the dark because those in control want to keep us in the dark.
BILLIE: *(Accusing him.)* You're interested in conspiracy theories.
ALVIN: My monument to conspiracy theories is going to have no planning to it. I'm just going to let it rip. Hopefully it'll be one of my greatest works.
BILLIE: Actually, it's going to be pretty small, won't it?
ALVIN: Yeah. *(Pause.)*
BILLIE: You're such a visionary.
ALVIN: You think so?
BILLIE: That was a joke.
ALVIN: Let's hope the joke's not on you.

*Long pause.*

BILLIE: Well, you're an artist.
ALVIN: *(Pleased to be referred to as an artist.)* Thank you.
BILLIE: I wish you weren't so melancholy. It's probably easier to talk with a depressive. *(Getting flustered.)* Depressed people don't create warped things so that future beings can criticize us. Depressed people don't think of the future. Or if, they do, maybe that's why they're... well, you're mixing me all up!

*Pause.*

ALVIN: Well, if you don't mind, I'll take this box of toothpicks and the glue and get to work.
BILLIE: The toothpicks cost eleven cents.
ALVIN: When I left for the war they cost eight cents.

*Toothpick Monuments*

BILLIE: It's Nineteen-nineteen now. *(Defensively.)* With the war, the prices went up.
ALVIN: *(Sarcastically.)* Yeah, what a surprise.
BILLIE: And the glue now costs fifteen cents.
ALVIN: Funny that the glue should cost more than the toothpicks.
BILLIE: Maybe.
ALVIN: *(Gets the money out of his pocket and pays.)* Thanks. Have a good day.

ALVIN *exits, on crutches.*

BILLIE: I'll do my best. *(Under her breath.)* These boys that leave home and come back from the army. What ideas get into their heads! *(Pause.)* The world's beginning again. *(She fervently believes this:)* The Great War was the war to end all wars. It has. It will. You can count on it. *(Pause.)* Poor boy.

## 9. At the Shrink's Office

*The therapist,* JOANNE, *can have a continental European accent of some kind. She is seated.*

KAREN: How did the earth, the solar system, the stars come to exist? What were they born from? Were they born from anything? Birth and death are two points that make us think, make us shake our head and say, someone else or something else has power? What kind of vantage point is the earth? How would things be different if we lived on an asteroid? *(Pause.)* Give us a name for what we see. Give us a name out of frustration. We have no idea how we got here, why we're here, how the universe got here, we have no idea what HERE is. *(Longer pause.)* That's why when we don't know, we say GOD knows. We have books in which God is said to speak. Not only do these books tell us that God is speaking to us, they say if you don't believe what God is saying, that you'll live in misery. Not only now, but for the rest of eternity. So you see the world has messages, threatening messages – aggressive advertising exists on even the spiritual plane. *(Pause.)* What is eternity, anyway? Isn't that possibly biting off more than we can chew? *(Longer pause.)* The phone rings. I want to answer it. I can't get to it. I shout at the unanswered phone: "I won't be able to come... because I'm stuck here. On Planet Earth at what we absurdly call a specific time and I'm busy with trying to coming to grips with what I am."
JOANNE: It sounds like you have a complex about existence.
KAREN: Thank you, doctor.
JOANNE: And from what you've just said, I believe you might have a problem with authority. You know the difference between right and wrong, correct?

KAREN: I'm not so sure any more.
JOANNE: Let's talk about it.

*Pause.* KAREN *takes a seat. Pause.*

KAREN: Technology is wrong.
JOANNE: But for some it is right.
KAREN: The clouds are right.
JOANNE: But for some they are wrong.
KAREN: The barking of a dog is right.
JOANNE: In some cases that could be wrong.
KAREN: The barking of a cat is wrong.
JOANNE: I'm glad we can finally agree on something.

*Pause.*

JOANNE: Some say I can be tough as a therapist.
KAREN: What do you mean?

*Pause.* JOANNE *decides a change in subject is in order. She rises from her seat and gets a paintbrush.*

JOANNE: Let's do some art therapy.
KAREN: *(Hesitant.)* Um...
JOANNE: I think you'd better. *(Pause.)* Now, take this brush.

*She gives her the brush.*

KAREN: It's not so big, is it?

JOANNE: All the more better for you to be able to express yourself. All the more better for less mess. *(Pause.)* Now, if some paint DOES get on your hands, then you've made a mistake. But it's not as bad as paint getting somewhere else – like on the floor. If you do that, you have to stop painting and clean the paint off right away. The paint must not be anywhere where it's no supposed to be. Even the handle of the paintbrush is to remain clean. This is the difference between right and wrong.
KAREN: Okay.
JOANNE: Now, if you see paint DRIPPING, you've got to take care of it at once. Be sure to check for drips every five minutes.
KAREN: Five minutes?
JOANNE: They take a while to form – especially around knobs. Those almost always have drips of paint around them. You wait, you'll see.
KAREN: Okay, okay.
JOANNE: The first coat was easy. It was quick to clean up after. But you're going to be doing the second coat. And that's in oil. That mean's it's a real pain to clean up after. It'll probably take you longer to clean up than to actually paint it.
KAREN: The first coat looks good.
JOANNE: I did it myself and I knew what I was doing. Now it's your turn. You do the second coat.
KAREN: I thought this was supposed to be art therapy. This isn't art.
JOANNE: That's a judgment left best for future generations. *(Pause.)* We focus on expressing ourselves.
KAREN: Art does more than that.

## At the Shrink's Office

JOANNE: My, my! You DO have problems. *(Pause.)* There's a real art to what you're about to do. I couldn't do the second coat because I didn't want to smell the fumes because I was pregnant. Luckily, the first coat was water-based.
KAREN: You're not pregnant anymore.
JOANNE: But I'm back at work and I don't have time to paint.
KAREN: The fumes may be harmful.
JOANNE: You can crack open the window.
KAREN: But how is this painting going to benefit me?
JOANNE: Therapy works in strange ways.
KAREN: *(Sarcastically.)* Just like God works in strange ways –
JOANNE: There you go again with your complex about authority. *(Pause.)* Now, let's start painting.
KAREN: Does the paint stink that much?
JOANNE: What do you mean?
KAREN: You said you didn't want to paint when you were pregnant.
JOANNE: The paint stinks no more than any other oil-based paint.
KAREN: I didn't come here to paint.
JOANNE: There are a million things going on. My husband is away on business so he can't paint and I don't have time and I can't keep the office empty so it can be painted. I have to stay in business or otherwise I go out of business. *(Pause.)* Just paint the cabinets. I'll have another patient do the rest.
KAREN: I didn't expect this.
JOANNE: That's why people have problems. They have false expectations.
KAREN: I don't feel so good about this.

JOANNE: Shh! Be quiet. The baby's sleeping. *(Pause.)* And one other thing. *(Pause.)* I need to go out shopping for a few minutes. The baby's in her room and if you hear her wake up, can you just put the paintbrush down and see if she's all right?
KAREN: I always wanted to have children myself.
JOANNE: See, we're getting somewhere already. See what art therapy does? *(Very impressed with her patient's progress. The following is spoken in the European language that is the "cause" of her foreign accent. Here for example, is the French:)* QUELLE RÉALISATION!
KAREN: What?
JOANNE: You've wanted to have children but you've never spoken it out loud.
KAREN: I have said it out loud. To many people.
JOANNE: To men?
KAREN: A few.
JOANNE: That's one of the ways you scared them away! *(Pause.)* Well, I'd better get going. *(Pause.)* One other thing. While I'm gone, if the baby cries and wants milk, give her some.
KAREN: Is there a warm bottle somewhere?
JOANNE: No. That's why I'm going out.
KAREN: Then what should I do?
JOANNE: Breastfeed her.
KAREN: I don't think I could do that.
JOANNE: What, are you some kind of prude?
KAREN: But I come to YOU for support! I have personal problems. Spiritual, intellectual and emotional problems.
JOANNE: A baby always comes first.
KAREN: It's not like I expected to come here and help breastfeed.
JOANNE: Well, maybe you DID.
KAREN: No, I didn't.

*At the Shrink's Office*

JOANNE: I don't see why you don't want to help.
KAREN: You're here to help me. That's why I'm paying you.
JOANNE: See how inadequate you are! The road to sane living is being able to help others regardless of money.
KAREN: I don't like painting. I've never done it for myself and I'm not going to do it for someone else.
JOANNE: There's no cure for you. You're too selfish. Someone offers you help and you reject it. There's nothing I can do for you.
KAREN: No, please, doctor, I do need help. But leaving me alone with the baby is exposing me to my weaknesses.
JOANNE: Overcome them.
KAREN: Maybe I'm just not ready.
JOANNE: Tell that to a baby who needs you!

KAREN *rises.*

KAREN: That's why I want a baby! I believe a baby will give me a reason to live. I believe a baby will give me someone to live for. It will give me structure.
JOANNE: You're pathetic.
KAREN: You have everything. A job. A husband. A baby. How dare you say I'm pathetic!
JOANNE: Okay, maybe I'm being a little rough. Look, we only have so much time. I need to do the shopping. Will you stop focusing on YOU long enough to get something done? The world keeps on going. It doesn't wait only for you. You're not the center of the universe.
KAREN: That's true. That's what I've been thinking for some time now. I've just been waiting for some context to make it all real.
JOANNE: I'm providing you with that context.

*A baby is heard. Pause.*

JOANNE: Hear that, the baby's crying. Go see if there's a problem.
KAREN: Yes, yes! I will. With pleasure. *(Pause.)* Wow, I'm starting to feel better already.
JOANNE: Just make sure to stir the paint thoroughly before you start. We don't want any lumps.
KAREN: Lumps...
JOANNE: I've got to get going.
KAREN: ...Stir the paint? But the baby?
JOANNE: LET HER CRY! We can't look in on her every time she lets out a whimper! You have to start painting. I'll see you in a half hour.
KAREN: Take as long as you need. *(Pause.)* I never expected to feel so good so fast!

*Pause. An echo is heard of what she said before*, KAREN: "I don't feel so good about this." *Then:*

KAREN: I never expected to feel so good so fast!

*Pause. Another echo is heard of what she said before*, KAREN: "I don't feel so good about this." *Then, immediately, once more:*

KAREN: I never expected to feel so good so fast!

## 10. Blast Off

AL *is alone. A glass of water is on a nearby table.* BOB *walks in on him.*

BOB: Al, We're too much alike. Each of us should have someone who's different.
AL: Different? How so?
BOB: To start with, we each should have a woman in our lives.
AL: I do have women in my life.
BOB: Yes, Al, but there's nothing serious...
AL: All my relationships are serious.
BOB: I mean, a woman that's a partner. *(Pause.)* It's not easy for either one of us, I know. Am I really only speaking for myself when I say that I'm not happy living alone? And I'm miserable because of where I work.
AL: You like your work. You meet beautiful models there every day.
BOB: Looks aren't everything.
AL: Well, I've heard they write poetry –
BOB: It's not very deep. *(Pause.)* I need to talk to a woman like I'm able to talk with you.
AL: We're lucky to have each other.
BOB: But it's not enough.
AL: It's not like we can go out and find somebody just like that. *(Pause.)* You've tried to cut your connection to me like this before.
BOB: This isn't a criticism of your humaneness.
AL: You're cutting and you're starting to run.
BOB: I owe it to you to tell you what I feel. We need lovers. I'd like to find someone, live with them.

AL: You've always lived alone. You don't really know how to be together with someone.
BOB: *(On the attack.)* Okay. You had lovers. They were odd women, we know that. So, what's it prove? That you've loved – IN YOUR OWN WAY – but you're not into long-term relationships.

*Long pause.*

BOB: We're going to die.
AL: *(Looking him up and down.)* So THAT'S what this is all about? You don't want to grow old and have no lover at your side. But you have me. I won't let you down.
BOB: You really want to be alone?
AL: I'm not alone. I have you.
BOB: What if something happens to me?
AL: I'll replace you with another person who's close to me.
BOB: Such a person is not easy to find.

*Long pause.*

BOB: I have to be honest with you. You depress me.
AL: *(Disbelieving.)* What?! You depress yourself. I'm here, keeping you stable. *(Pause.)* I can't possibly depress you anymore than Mother, or our sister.
BOB: You never told me that Susan depressed you.
AL: She doesn't. I'm just saying that she depresses you.
BOB: Oh.
AL: Her husband can get me down, though. And her kids, sometimes.

*Blast Off*

BOB: Those kids are no different than others *(Facial gesture indicates he's a bit in the dark about that.)* – from what I hear. Aren't all kids like them?
AL: They're not, but you, Bob, wouldn't have anyway of knowing that. *(Pause.)* The depression you have is worrisome.
BOB: When I'm depressed, there's always a reason.
AL: *(Disbelieves him, has heard this before from him.)* Your case is one where the depression is a due to a biochemical imbalance rather than an emotional problem.
BOB: How can you say that?
AL: Because I'm a board-certified psychiatrist. *(Pause.)* I doubt you'll find anyone who can understand your problems as well as I can.
BOB: I need to break it off with you.
AL: Let me tell you this: if we break it off, I'll never talk to you again. It would be too complicated to do that. And it would be too expensive. Because if we broke it off, I'd just have to... go back to Earth. And even with what a psychiatrist makes, flying back to Earth from Mars is a once-in-a-lifetime expense.
BOB: You'd be happy to move away, because you feel that our family is a tiny speck of a soap opera in the universe.
AL: No, I'm afraid that's how YOU feel. Listen. Life is hard here because Mars presents very stressful challenges to the human body... and mind. I'm needed here, even more than I am on Earth. But if I'm not appreciated, I'll go. *(Changing his mind.)* Maybe... maybe YOU should go back to Earth, if you want to be rid of me.
BOB: I'm staying. This is the land where our father died, bringing water back into the canals.
AL: And look how you spit on his memory.
BOB: Nothing of the kind!

• 59

AL: He said we must live together and if we don't, we'll all fall together. Look, there's only seven of us on all of Mars! I administer to the entire family's needs; let me go down the list:
One: There's Mother; she's kept sane by me and her pets, especially the cats.
Two: There's you; you know how much I'm there for you. Even though you deny that you like your job as C.E.O. of the water company.
Three: Susan. As a mother of two beautiful teenage girls, you know very well her stresses
Four: John, her husband. He's taken over for father. Chief Hydro Engineer. ONLY engineer... on the PLANET!
Five: Antonia. She models in front of the canals. To make sure the water looks attractive to buyers on Earth.
Six: Josephine, her younger and prettier sister; always trying to take modeling assignments away from her.
Seven: There's me. What if I go? Our family and civilization are placed in great, great danger.
*(Pause.)* But if you're really thinking that we should no longer be close, let me tell you this – it's been a secret until now:
*(Pause.)* Mother had other lovers. Before Dad.
BOB: So what.
AL: I'm not Dad's biological son.
BOB: How would you know that?

*AL continues to play the authoritative psychiatrist and rather less of the brother.*

AL: I'm the eldest. Dad confided in me. Before he died.
BOB: *(Finds in this grounds for some kind of hope.)* So we're not quite as alike as I thought we were!

AL: No.
BOB: *(Confused but upset, too.)* What does this mean?
AL: And another thing...
BOB: *(Overwhelmed.)* No! I don't want to hear anymore!
AL: Susan, your sister... she's my... daughter!
BOB: No! No! *(Pause.)* But why should I care? Does that really affect me? *(Pause.)* Yes, it does! Because you had sex with our mother and you killed my father. You vile scum!
AL: No, Susan's mother was a girlfriend of mine.
BOB: But you were on Mars by then!
AL: There was another woman that lived here besides Mother.
BOB: Really?
AL: Her name was Lilly. She was Dad's mistress.
BOB: So you had sex with the same woman that Dad did?
AL: That is correct.
BOB: That's disgusting.
AL: No, it gets worse. Mom was through with her lovers. They were relegated to the distant past. However, when she found out that Dad had a lover, and I had that same lover, and that the lover, Lilly - you're following me, right? - gave birth to Susan, well... Mother flew into a rage.
BOB: What?!
AL: She killed Lilly. And there wasn't a thing I could do about it except become a psychiatrist.
BOB: It's so twisted here!
AL: *(Showing off his brilliance.)* Yes, it is - space is warped, just like it is everywhere. Relativity isn't a theory, it's reality. Ha! And you want to leave me behind!
BOB: I want a woman. You've had a woman. Me... no!
AL: It's not all it's cracked up to be.

BOB: But I'm lonely.
AL: No, you're just depressed.

AL *offers* BOB *a glass of water.*

BOB: I don't want your drugs.
AL: At least drink some water.
BOB: How do I know you haven't spiked it?
AL: You have to trust me.
BOB: I can't trust anybody on this red planet.
AL: *(Pause.)* Listen, Bob, where can you find a woman here?
BOB: You're right. There's no one... extra.
AL: You're thinking straighter now.
BOB: I'll have that water.

BOB *drinks from the glass. He pauses.*

BOB: I want to kill you.
AL: How will that get you a woman?
BOB: I want to kill you. Because you killed my father.
AL: Oh, come off it!
BOB: You slept with Lilly and made our sister.
AL: That's true. Then Mom killed Lilly and Dad died a natural death!
BOB: He did not. Lilly killed him.
AL: Lilly was already dead. You're talking nonsense.
BOB: Prove it!
AL: Drink more water! Come to your senses!

*Blast Off*

*Pause.* BOB *drinks more water. He is then a bit more relaxed.*

BOB: Is this what sexual frustration is about?
AL: Partly.
BOB: Partly? Why can't I ever get a clear, unequivocal answer from you?
AL: Nothing is clear and unequivocal.
BOB: Spare me your relativism!
AL: The truth is how we see things on a certain day.
BOB: I don't believe that.
AL: See, that's another difference between us.
BOB: You don't believe that either. Stop. Stop playing with my mind. You're so sadistic! Never have a psychiatrist for a brother!
AL: Half-brother.
BOB: You always have to qualify everything you say!
AL: *(Pause, then:)* Here we are, on a planet our race doesn't come from. Our original planet has been taken over by apes. You've read the history books, right?
BOB: Yes, "Planet of the Apes".
AL: Of course I don't want to go back there to the few humans who are left... they're in cages or in wild zones where they hide among the trees...
BOB: That's why *I* should go. I'm going to get into that spaceship, *(He points to somewhere offstage.)* and find myself a woman!
AL: It's your life, though you should think of others.
BOB: I need to think of me.
AL: You're going back to Earth?
BOB: No, I'm going to Venus. You know there's a colony there,

AL: But they don't speak our language.
BOB: I'll learn.
AL: But the beings there don't have hands or feet. You won't find them sexually attractive.
BOB: I'll get used to them. I'll adapt.
AL: But they have three different sexes there, and none of them are female!
BOB: I'll transform them. Man has great transformative gifts. Look what Dad did here!
AL: Man has his limits.
BOB: I know no limits!
AL: Then you are tragic.
BOB: No, I'm just horny!
AL: You just have an obsession, that's all.
BOB: Call it what ever you want, Doctor.
AL: You should calm down. I suggest you keep a daily journal.
BOB: I will – in outer space! *(Pause.)* You remember Dad – he had a temper like me...
AL: Sometimes he got pretty wound up.
BOB: Well... passion got him to this planet and passion will get me THROUGH TO VENUS! *(Pause.)* It's so liberating knowing that you've shed your family and you're going to have a new one.
AL: The liberation will wear off.
BOB: You're just trying to have me not leave.
AL: Go. If you must.
BOB: We're not alike! What a revelation it's been for me to find that out! I'm very, very free!
AL: It's a wonderful feeling, isn't it?

*Blast Off*

BOB: *(Pauses. Reflects.)* And horrible, too. We humans can't help it. There's sadness in our genetic makeup.
AL: In yours. I've been trying to tell you that.
BOB: I don't want your drugs. I'm getting in the spaceship.
AL: Good, then do it.
BOB: First I have to say goodbye to Mom. *(Pause.)* No, wait, I'm not going to do that, or I'll never leave. Give her this kiss from me.

BOB *seizes* AL *and kisses him with intense youthful passion on the lips.*

AL: *(Recovers, then:)* I will. *(Pause.)* You're really going to go?
BOB: Yes.
AL: Well, look, ah... before you go. *(Pause.)* There's something I should mention to you. Dad left something. For you... in case you were thinking of going... It's a female. She's a robot. But she's really close to the real thing.
BOB: How do you know that?
AL: Because I...
BOB: Why do you always get there first!?
AL: Because I was born first. You have to accept that.
BOB: *(Bitterly.)* I'll take your girl robot!
AL: Good, you'll stay here then, with your new lover and the rest of us.
BOB: No. She'll be in the seat next to me in the spaceship *(He gestures to the spaceship that is just offstage.)* as we wing our way to Venus.
AL: Why do you need to go? You have your woman now.

• 65

BOB: *(A big speech.)* Man is born insecure. He needs to do things that make him feel big. It's man's destiny to explore the stars! He can't know himself unless he achieves something outside himself. He can't be stopped by fantasies where robots replace reality because a brother...
AL: Half-brother.
BOB: ... thinks he should stay! Forget dreams... I must establish a place that's fundamentally NEW. I must do something that shows that I am slave to no one. Dad did it. I'm doing it.
AL: I can't believe you're going. You said you only wanted a woman.
BOB: Where's the robot?
AL: Come on, I'll show you. Hey, you know, she's better than a real woman. She never complains.
BOB: Well, I have a complaint. With the cosmos. This is what I say: I'm not happy and I, I will change that! Where is that dirty robot, that whore!?

## 11. After One Glass of Wine

BRENDA *and* ALEX *sit at a restaurant table for two.*

BRENDA: You don't know how much I love you.
ALEX: You've told me before that you love me – many times. So...
BRENDA: Yeah, but HOW much I love you... have I told you how much?
ALEX: Maybe not as thoroughly as you would like – I'm just guessing at that.
BRENDA: How much do you love me?
ALEX: Oh, you're changing the subject.
BRENDA: You're right. *(To herself also:)* Yeah, what made me do that? *(Pause. Answering.)* I know. I wanted to hear you say the word "love."
ALEX: You like the sound of the word love –
BRENDA: I love the sound of your voice, too.
ALEX: It's a positive sounding word – love.
BRENDA: "Positive?"
ALEX: It's not negative, is it?
BRENDA: True. *(Pause.)* How much positive?
ALEX: There's no "how much" in positive. Something's either positive or negative.
BRENDA: Then why do people say they're "very positive" about something?
ALEX: They're emphasizing positive – incorrectly, actually. Positive is positive and negative is negative.
BRENDA: No gradations?
ALEX: Not really.

BRENDA: If things were just positive or negative – or black and white – with nothing in between – it wouldn't be a very pretty world. When I say I love you very much and I say I want to say more than that it's obvious that I'd like to say something more descriptive, something that'll describe how much... something that'll give life to our love, something that'll make it real and exciting...
ALEX: Something special...
BRENDA: Yeah, something special, something that gives it character and COLOR. *(Pause.)* You know, "fabulous" is a more exciting word than "positive".
ALEX: They're different words.
BRENDA: You're in an enviable position. Someone's struggling to tell you how much they love YOU.
ALEX: Don't think I'm not grateful for it. But don't envy me. Just be happy for me. Be happy for you. Be happy for us.
BRENDA: Happy. Have you ever noticed that the great poets never use that word?
ALEX: I never noticed that.
BRENDA: They don't use it because they're looking for something more expressive.
ALEX: They don't use "fabulous" very much.
BRENDA: *(Pause.)* I have a tough time with words.
ALEX: Your efforts are admirable. They're touching.
BRENDA: I don't use words well.
ALEX: Well, what other people do is they don't tell each other how much they love each other. They don't say "love" except quickly, without thinking much – like when they leave, or they end a letter or a card...
BRENDA: I don't want to be like other people who say "love" real quick and probably don't mean it most of the time. Just think of the English. They always say "love". Like, thanks for coming into my shop, love, to buy some new carpet and glue!

*After One Glass of Wine*

ALEX: They're not saying love spelled l-o-v-e. They're saying luv, spelled l-u-v.
BRENDA: But when it's coming out of their mouths it's still "love" and they don't mean it! *(Pause.)* You don't say love enough to me because you don't really love me.
ALEX: That's not true at all! *(Pause.)* So that's what this is about. You think I don't love you.
BRENDA: You let me assume that everything's fabulous between us. *(Commands him.)* Tell me flat out that your love for me is as great as the day is long – or something like that.
ALEX: But the length of the day changes every day.
BRENDA: I can deal with that. The point is the greatness.
ALEX: My love for you is as great as the day is long.
BRENDA: No. *I* said that. You come up with something original.

*Pause.*

BRENDA: Well?
ALEX: I'm thinking.
BRENDA: You don't really love me! And that's just like me – to have something beautiful to say and give it away, before I realize I've thrown it away!
ALEX: But you didn't throw it away. I used it.
BRENDA: But *I* wanted to use it! It's just like a woman to think of something and have a man take it and make it his!
ALEX: Sorry.
BRENDA: You're not sorry. I always help you out of tough spots! Without me you'd be embarrassed that you didn't have anything really romantic to say.
ALEX: Thanks for helping me out.

BRENDA: I didn't mean to. But I'm a woman. That's just the way it is. I should have never tried to express my feelings to you.
ALEX: Your heart is in the right place.
BRENDA: What kind of namby-pamby statement is that?
ALEX: I'm just trying to make you feel better.
BRENDA: Oh, you're trying to make me "happy". Maybe we should review our relationship.
ALEX: It looks like we've already started doing that. *(Pause.)* Anybody's asking for trouble they start talking abstractly. My high school teacher said that most students discover too late that their essays are easier to write if they stick to what is more concrete.
BRENDA: *(Sarcastically.)* Concrete? That's romantic. Maybe we should call up your high school teacher right now.
ALEX: I think the point was how to avoid getting lost while writing an essay. *(Pause.)* Look, we're fairly normal people. You're not Superwoman, I'm not Superman and neither of us is a poet.
BRENDA: You don't understand women. We want more than your silent "love".
ALEX: Okay.

ALEX's *attention drifts. He might be looking at a waitress.*

BRENDA: We want to talk. We want understanding. *(Pause.)* Pay attention to me. What were you just looking at? Were you looking at that waitress?
ALEX: No.
BRENDA: You were looking at that waitress!
ALEX: I was not.

*After One Glass of Wine*

BRENDA: You only want sex. With as many women as possible!
ALEX: I don't like the new direction of this conversation.
BRENDA: Oh, it's a "conversation"? Is that all it is!?

*He does not answer.*

BRENDA: I'm not Superwoman, but I'm a woman.
ALEX: Right.
BRENDA: Don't tell me "right".
ALEX: Look. I love you. Very much. My love for you is as great as the distance between the moon and the stars.
BRENDA: Stop. Don't try to manipulate me!
ALEX: I'm not.
BRENDA: You are.
ALEX: Hmph!
BRENDA: What's that?

*(Pause.)*

BRENDA: That's a grunt. Don't grunt me.
ALEX: Hmph!
BRENDA: Yeah, that expresses it all. CAVE MAN. You can find yourself a hotel room in another cave tonight! You're not sleeping in the same bed with me!
ALEX: What?
BRENDA: Oh, he speaks. *(Pause.)* Someone's either RIGHT for you or WRONG for you. There's no in between. We're just not for each other. To me it looks pretty black and white!

## 12. Bats

*In a police station.* AND *is an informant and is talking to policeman/woman* BUT, *who sits at a desk.* BUT *sometimes takes notes.*

AND: They made a barbecue. They were eating and talking. They talked about tattoos. He's got several. She has one.
BUT: But did you see them using drugs?
AND: It was starting to get dark. The bats started to come out.
BUT: You said there were woods around the picnic table. Bats like the open air.
AND: The woods were only on one side. So there was plenty of open air.
BUT: And you were listening... from where?
AND: I told you there was a big boulder on the right and I was behind it.
BUT: You're sure you didn't see them using drugs.
AND: I'm sure.
BUT: And you weren't using.
AND: No.
BUT: Continue.
AND: Well, the bats started flying around. They were so fast I couldn't believe it. I thought I'd be safe if I just stayed where I was. But one of them slammed right into my forehead.
BUT: Ouch.
AND: Yeah.
BUT: Now you told the first officer you spoke with that you were hit by a bat out of Hell.
AND: That's correct, officer.
BUT: How do you know the bat was coming out of Hell?

AND: There are caves in that park.
BUT: Yes.
AND: The caves lead to Hell.
BUT: The maps that we've been looking at show no indication of that.
AND: They don't put Hell on maps.
BUT: Ours are top quality geological survey maps. Maps don't get any better than that.
AND: Mapmakers don't want to scare anybody. That's why they leave Hell off. Have you ever seen Hell on any map?
BUT: No.
AND: That answers the question.
BUT: You're the one who's supposed to answer the questions. You could've been hit by just any old bat. Or, more likely, maybe the people you were spying on threw something at you.
AND: No, they couldn't see me.
BUT: I don't know why you think the bat came from Hell.
AND: Because of its speed and its smell.
BUT: What'd it smell like?
AND: Fire. And brimstone.
BUT: What is brimstone?
AND: You're not a Christian?
BUT: That's not any of your business. *(Pause.)* Have you ever smelled a normal bat?
AND: Don't try to tell me that Hell doesn't exist.
BUT: Answer the question please. What does a normal bat smell like?
AND: I don't know.
BUT: Then how do you know what a bat out of Hell smells like?

AND: It wasn't the smell of bats, it was the smell of fire and brimstone!
BUT: Are you sure you weren't smelling their barbecue?
AND: I'm sure.
BUT: Maybe they threw at hot dog at you.
AND: I told you, they didn't see me.
BUT: Why do you think a bat from Hell would fly into YOU?
AND: Maybe by mistake.
BUT: Maybe not by mistake.
AND: Oh, you mean, maybe I was being punished for being a rat?
BUT: I didn't say that. *(Pause.)* What you're doing for us is important.
AND: Then why are you trying to make me feel guilty?
BUT: You are guilty. You have a criminal record that goes back twenty years. You often violate the conditions of your parole. *(Pause.)* Now, I'm sorry you experienced what you did. We've taken notes on what you've said and even done some preliminary investigation into where the bat came from. *(Pause.)* There's not a lot more I can do. But what WE can do is bring Rafael Massena in off the street. We need eyewitnesses that see him selling cocaine.
AND: I didn't see any of that.
BUT: Maybe next time you will. *(Pause.)* You know, part of the deal of you staying out of jail is helping us out.
AND: I'm trying.
BUT: Good.
AND: But it's the smell, man! The smell! You never forget it when Hell hits you.
BUT: Take a shower.
AND: No, the smell stays in your memory.

BUT: That's what we're counting on. Your memory. *(Trying once more, knowing it is in vain.)* Are you sure you don't remember seeing him sell that musician woman some cocaine?
AND: I never saw or heard anything about cocaine. They seemed to be on a date, in a park, having a barbecue. *(Pause. Pretty scared:)* What am I going to do about the smell?!
BUT: There's only so much we can do for you. I guess you'll have to somehow get over it. *(Pause.)* You can go now.
AND: *(Muttering.)* Man, it's horrible!

AND *leaves.*

BUT: This job is hard. These informants... are a joke. I know that park – where they had that picnic. It's near the caves. Those caves DO lead to Hell.

*Pause.* BUT *gets up from the desk and approaches the audience and speaks to the audience directly.*

BUT: Those bats are always in a hurry. Not because they're coming out of Hell and it's too hot for them there. No, they're moving fast because they got only so much time to get into the air of this world where there's a lot more space. So they can play in it, like dolphins. *(Pause.)* Then they go back to Hell and say, "Look, I visit upstairs every night. It ain't so much different than here, 'cept that the people there are confused and don't know what to do with themselves. They get into all sorts of trouble 'coz of it... *(Pause.)* Down here, well, nobody's confused. *(Pause.)* Sure, they're in trouble. But they know WHY."

• 75

## 13. Spaghetti

*In addition to the boss* LOU *and an employee,* MARTY, *there is a third character that has not been notated in the dialog below. Let us call this third character* "MANDY". *Let's say that* MANDY *is a competitive type, and wants to outshine* MARTY *at the company.*

*This third character* MANDY *always "simultaneously" (the actor tries as best as they can) says what* MARTY *says, but* MANDY *adds, at the very end of each* "MARTY" *speech, the word* "boss". *Here is an example of what* MANDY *will say – a speech that has more than one sentence has been intentionally chosen to demonstrate the point:*

MANDY: Right. *(Pause.)* But ...spaghetti is sold by weight, boss.

*Thus, before* LOU *answers or speaks again,* LOU *will have to wait to hear the word,* "boss".

MANDY's *changing inflections and timings of the word "boss" will vary, at times bringing about a humorous result.*

MARTY *will be irritated from time to time by* MANDY's *brownnosing.*

*The action of the sketch is set in the boss's office.*

LOU: Do you realize what can happen if we shorten our spaghetti? Nobody's going to notice a difference of one centimeter. Or maybe a whole inch.
MARTY: Yeah, like who ever said that spaghetti had to be a certain length?

*Spaghetti*

LOU: Exactly. Like, there's no law.
MARTY: Right. *(Pause.)* But ...spaghetti is sold by weight.
LOU: So we put it in a thicker, heavier box. Make a chic box.
MARTY: The box could wind up being more expensive than the spaghetti.
LOU: You've raised a legitimate point. *(Pause.)* Okay, we'll keep the cardboard the same weight. The spaghettis will be at least one centimeter shorter – and on the outside of the box we'll say, something like "contains 150 strands."
MARTY: Strands? Is that what you call a piece of spaghetti?
LOU: We certainly can't call them "noodles". That sounds low-rent.
MARTY: It sounds low-rent, yeah.
LOU: We'll get people used to thinking in terms of spaghetti being available in strands – not by the ounce or pound. It's easy to do with macaroni, too. Think of the money we can save. That means money earned!
MARTY: This is going to revolutionize pasta!
LOU: *(Proudly.)* Yeah.
MARTY: What do we call the little pieces of macaroni? "Strands" doesn't really fit.
LOU: Let me think... A single macaroni is... a SPLETA. That sounds Italian enough. And... let's call a single spaghetti, a DURATA. *(Pause.)* Forget "strands" – it has no ring to it! *(Pause.)* I'll have my people call the pasta factory right away and get them to adjust the machines. *(Pause.)* You get the people at the packaging plant to shrink the boxes and change the wording. *(Pause.)* Things like this have been done with so many other products. I don't know why nobody's ever noticed what could be done with pasta. Why is that?

MARTY *does not, or cannot answer the question.*

LOU: It's because they're stuck in the rut of weighing dry, uncooked food.
MARTY: You mean, SPLETAS of macaroni and DURATAS of spaghetti.
LOU: *(Smiling.)* Yeah.

*There may be a problem.*

MARTY: But counting pasta might make the customer conscious of something we don't want them to be conscious of.
LOU: Like what?
MARTY: They may eat fewer duratas, or spletas. Like, they go on a diet, and suddenly, you know, they buy less. . .
LOU: Well, then, we'll have even smaller boxes of duratas for them. And increase the price – because it's... "Dietetic".

*Pause.*

LOU: To think I never went to one of those fancy business schools at an Ivy League college. I've come up with something so brilliant! Why am I so brilliant? Is it something I inherited from my parents, one a Mexican peasant who only ate beans and rice, and the other, a seal-eating Eskimo from the north fishing grounds of Lapland? *(Pause.)* Is it hereditary... or is it the business environment of this country? *(Pause.)* Nature or Nurture?
MARTY: Yes, a classic "either-or".

*Spaghetti*

Lou: A valid question open to endless discussion. But this much is certain: though the Chinese invented capitalism, WE'RE the ones who have actually PURIFIED it and shown that it's the only economic system that keeps us all free.
Marty: Those are very heady thoughts. You are very brilliant. It's a combination of your own genius, your parents' genius, ...the genius of America... AND MY GENIUS, TOO!
Lou: You know, I used to live in a socialist country – Canada. There's no genius there. How can there be? There's no room for it. It's all about the group!

*Pause.*

Lou: You know what really helps me in all this?
Marty: What?
Lou: My detachment.
Marty: Detachment? What do you mean?
Lou: Pasta. No one in my family ever touches it. We don't like it. We don't eat it.
Marty: I can't stand the taste of it, either.

## 14. The Bee Farm

*A large old wooden tool shed is nearby.* BARRY *is dressed for farm work in blue jeans and a white tee shirt. He stands.* ANGELA *sits on a thick wooden slab that is a kind of makeshift bench. She wears "country clothes" but they are still very stylish. There is something exaggerated about* ANGELA's *femininity.*

BARRY: When I was eighteen, I was the guy you see in front of you right now.
ANGELA: You haven't changed since then?
BARRY: I changed. But I changed BACK. At one point I weighed five hundred pounds. Then I had my stomach stapled.
ANGELA: You were FAT once?
BARRY: I was morbidly obese. Most of my body was pure lard. For twelve years diets didn't do anything.
ANGELA: I would never have known. And you look so young.
BARRY: As long as they were doing gastric bypass surgery I had them do my face and neck. *(Pause.)* But let's not talk about surgery! That's what old people do.

*A pause.*

BARRY: People who are "with it" PARTICIPATE in life – they don't just observe it – like I did when I was fat.

ANGELA *is still surprised at the amazing journey that* BARRY *has been through during the past years.*

ANGELA: Wow!
BARRY: I don't usually bring up the old days except when I get nervous. I start talking. *(Pause.)* Boy, I could really use this job! *(Pause.)* Don't tell him what I told you. *(Pause.)* I don't mean to be nervous around you, sorry.
ANGELA: I guess your experiences make you a little afraid of the opposite sex.
BARRY: I'm more comfortable now. No more porn flicks anymore.

*An awkward pause.*

ANGELA: Maybe I shouldn't say this, but I don't have anything against pornography.
BARRY: Do you know that forty percent of the people who watch porn are woman?
ANGELA: Oh, really?

*BARRY does not want to talk about pornographic films. He regrets he brought the subject up.*

BARRY: You know, you're pretty. I don't know why a girl like you has go out for a job like this.
ANGELA: The bad economy's made jobs hard to come by. *(Pause.)* When I saw Dale Blankman's Bee Farm was looking for people to gather honey, I thought: why not give it a try?
BARRY: Me, too.

*Pause.*

BARRY: I wonder when Blankman's going to get here. It wasn't very nice of him to say be here by eight o'clock, and then he's not here when we show up.
ANGELA: Have you ever worked on a farm before?
BARRY: Nope. But... like you, *(They both need jobs.)* I'll try anything.
ANGELA: It could be interesting work. *(She appreciates the outdoors.)* We're outside.

*Pause.*

ANGELA: They say that fat people are jolly. Were you jolly when you were overweight?

*This is the wrong kind of question to ask* BARRY. *He really doesn't want to talk about once being fat.*

BARRY: Not really. People could be cruel. You know what some people called me?
ANGELA: No.
BARRY: Snowflake.

ANGELA *does not understand what is cruel about that.*

ANGELA: Yeah, so?
BARRY: A snowflake weighs nothing. I weighed almost five hundred pounds. Get it?

*Pause.*

Barry: You seem like a nice girl, if you don't mind me saying. Are you single?
Angela: Um. Still looking for Mister Right, if you must know.

*Barry feels uncomfortable and apologizes.*

Barry: Look, I didn't mean to pry, and I don't mean to talk so much – sorry.
Angela: What else are we going to do but talk? Farmer Blankman's not here yet.

*A pause. It's a beautiful morning. The air is clean. The sky sparkles. It is fresh blue, with a few high white clouds. The morning may be beautiful, but it is boring. After a while,* Angela *speaks:*

Angela: I guess we'll have to wear beekeeper suits.
Barry: Yeah.

*Like* Angela, Barry *finds it difficult to remain silent. He talks out of nervousness. He really shouldn't say what he says next but he is just trying to make conversation.*

Barry: I ask you this as a woman: do YOU watch porn?
Angela: Watch it?...

*Pause.*

Angela: Well, as long as you told me your secret about being fat, I'll tell you mine.

*Pause.*

ANGELA: I used to act in porno flicks. In fact, THIS job is my first job outside the adult entertainment industry.
BARRY: Really!?
ANGELA: I hope saying that doesn't like... make it hard for us to work together.
BARRY: *(It is not a problem for him.)* No.
ANGELA: I've slept with five hundred men.
BARRY: Naw!
ANGELA: A hundred million people have seen my private parts.
BARRY: God. Do I know you?
ANGELA: I used to go by the name Angela Angel.
BARRY: It doesn't ring a bell.

ANGELA *is relieved that she has told her secret and feels that she has been accepted by* BARRY.

ANGELA: I can breathe a little easier now.

BARRY *thinks for a moment. He remembers something.*

BARRY: Wait a second. Angela Angel? I know who that is! You're not a woman. *(Pause. Disgusted.)* You're a man! Who takes female hormones!
ANGELA: When's Blankman going to show up?

ANGELA'S *cell phone rings. She takes it out of her pocket and answers it.*

*The Bee Farm*

ANGELA: *(On phone.)* Hello. Oh, hi, Mr. Blankman. *(Pause.)* Yes, I'm here... and he is, too. *(Long pause while Blankman explains something over the phone. Then* ANGELA *speaks into the phone.)* The shed's unlocked? *(Phone to her ear, echoing the instructions so* BARRY *knows)* We can go ahead and put the beekeeper suits on. *(Pause.)* We won't be touching the beehives. *(Listening, still repeating the instructions.)* ...First thing is to clean up the bee manure. We'll see the shovels and bags for that.

*Pause.*

ANGELA: *(Still on phone.)* Okay, it sounds simple enough. We'll see you in a half hour.

ANGELA *hangs up her phone and puts it away.*

BARRY: What happened?
ANGELA: He also owns a turkey farm. Last night was a full moon. They laid lots of eggs. He's going to be late.
BARRY: Oh.
ANGELA: So you got what he said?

BARRY *does not answer her question.*

BARRY: I have to be honest. I'm a little weirded-out by you. I don't think I can work with you.
ANGELA: What, SNOWFLAKE, do you have something against transsexuals?
BARRY: Generally, um, people like you make me want to puke.
ANGELA: *(Upset, to herself, frustrated.)* I'm just trying to get a normal job!

• 85

BARRY: Maybe you should have stayed where you were.
ANGELA: YOU changed. Well, *I* changed.
BARRY: You're not a woman. You're...
ANGELA: Okay, FAT BOY. I can defend myself. Put 'em up!

ANGELA *raises her hands, makes two fists and starts to move her hands and feet like a boxer in a ring.* BARRY *takes up the challenge. He starts moving like a boxer in a ring. They move their hands and feet, sparring. They circle around in the imaginary boxing ring.*

BARRY: *(Moving, sparring.)* You don't scare me.
ANGELA: *(Moving, sparring.)* You're scared. You still play with rubber duckies in the bathtub, you little baby.
BARRY: *(Moving, sparring.)* I don't take baths. I shower.
ANGELA: *(Moving, sparring, trying land a punch.)* Couch potato. Snowflake!
BARRY: *(Moving, punching back.)* Fairy. Transvestite!
ANGELA: *(Moving, sparring.)* I'm not a transvestite. I'm transsexual. I'll teach you to get it right. I'll scratch your eyes out!
BARRY: You think you can scratch out my eyes!

ANGELA *has a change of heart. Suddenly she stops boxing and moves a short distance from* BARRY. BARRY *stops moving.*

ANGELA: This is no way to start the first day. We're not going to get any money if we don't work.
BARRY: I hate you.
ANGELA: I hate you, too. We'd better get the bee suits out of the shed.
BARRY: All right.

*They go over to the shed and open the door. A swarm of bees flies out of the shed and wastes no time in getting close to* ANGELA *and* BARRY *who are taken completely by surprise.*

ANGELA: Oh, no, there's bees!

*The bees go after them both.*

BARRY: How'd the bees get in there?
ANGELA: I don't know.

*They swat at the bees. Then after a while:*

BARRY: They're supposed to be in their hives.
ANGELA: I guess they just wanted to be free.

*A bee stings* ANGELA.

ANGELA: Ow!
BARRY: If we swat at them they're only going to attack us more.

*Another bee stings* ANGELA.

ANGELA: Oh no, they stung me again! *(Pause.)* I'm getting stung all over!

*The bee venom starts to affect* ANGELA.

ANGELA: My head's spinning! *(She has trouble breathing.)* I'm having a reaction. I can't breathe. *(Choking.)* I'm going to die.

ANGELA *falls to the ground.*

BARRY: What? *(Finding it hard to believe.)* Is it THAT bad? *(Pause.)* You're not going to die.
ANGELA: Oxygen. I need oxygen! *(Pause.)* Quick, now!
BARRY: *(Pause.)* What do you mean? *(Pause.)* What do I do?
ANGELA: Mouth-to-mouth resuscitation!

BARRY *is repulsed.*

BARRY: I can't do that!
ANGELA: You want me to die?
BARRY: No.
ANGELA: You're going to kill me if you don't.

ANGELA *writhes on the ground.*

BARRY: I can't let you die. You're right. *(He pauses. he thinks to himself.)* Now's not the time to have prejudices. Sure, I think you're REALLY WEIRD and the thought of touching you makes my skin crawl, but, hey, YOUR life hasn't been easy—taking hormones and being in adult movies and then trying leave that business. My life's been no picnic either! I should have some compassion.
ANGELA: Yes, stop thinking! Show some compassion!
BARRY: *(Continuing to think aloud.)* So, you're different. The world's diverse! If one thinks everybody should BE the same, LOOK the same, we'll they're living in a FOOL'S PARADISE!

*The idea that he has to perform mouth-to-mouth resuscitation on her just does not settle well with him.*

BARRY: I never kissed a man before, I never DREAMED of kissing a man before. This could leave life-long scars!
ANGELA: *(In agony.)* But think of the scars you'll have because I died and you could've saved me!
BARRY: You're right, there's no argument there. *(Going through the process in his mind, trying to picture it.)* I have to give you oxygen with my mouth. Maybe there's a tube lying around here somewhere.

ANGELA *is suffocating from the effects of the bee poison.*

ANGELA: A tube? No. There's no time!
BARRY: See, if I used a tube, I wouldn't have to touch your mouth.
ANGELA: But what if I don't have enough energy to close my lips around the end of the tube?
BARRY: You've had plenty of practice. All those dicks you've sucked!

*Pause.*

BARRY: Ugh! I can't get the image out of my mind!
ANGELA: I don't do that anymore. I've changed. Save me!
BARRY: I remember when I was fat. Nobody could save me but myself.
ANGELA: You had doctors! Look, I can't save myself. Bee poison is flooding my system. My lungs are paralyzed. I CAN'T BREATHE IN!

ANGELA *frantically tries to take in short breaths.*

BARRY: We just had a fight where you called me some awful names.
ANGELA: You called me some, too.

*Pause.*

ANGELA: *(In agony, and gasping.)* Are you waiting for Farmer Blankman to get here to do something, or what? If you are, then I'll be dead. *(Starts to weep.)* No one cares about me!
BARRY: That's just the way I felt.
ANGELA: Do something!

*Looking her up and down.*

BARRY: You know, you're not so bad looking—for a half-man.
ANGELA: *(In agony.)* Now's not the time to express a change in sexual tolerance!
BARRY: *(Looks around him.)* There's no tube here. *(He makes a stupid, bad, macho joke.)* The only tube I've got is in my pants!
ANGELA: You're sicker than I ever was.
BARRY: You're still alive so don't use the word, "was". That's the past tense.
ANGELA: Okay! So I made a grammar mistake! You'd make a few if your brain was shutting down because of the bee venom in it!

BARRY *swats some bees away. But he gets stung.*

BARRY: Oh, no. The bees have stung me, too! I'm feeling woozy. I'm going to faint!
ANGELA: You can't faint. You have to give me oxygen!
BARRY: I'm not going to make it either!
ANGELA: I've got a plan. First you resuscitate me, and then I'll resuscitate you. Look, maybe you were fat because you didn't know anything about cooperation.
BARRY: What's knowing about cooperation got to do with anything?!
ANGELA: There was a LACK of cooperation. You just sat in a chair ALONE, throwing food down your throat!
BARRY: It was better than what you put down your throat. *(Taunting her.)* You know a lot about cooperating, I'm sure!

*More bees sting* BARRY.

ANGELA: *(Being genuine, in earnest, though still gasping.)* I'll teach you cooperation. It'll be a lesson that'll save your life.
BARRY: *(Dizzy, desperate. Almost out of breath.)* I guess there's no other choice.

*Completely by chance there is a short piece of plastic tubing that has been in the grass near them.*

BARRY: *(Surprised.)* Well, look at that! There's a piece of tube!

BARRY *picks this piece of tube and wastes no time in giving mouth-to-mouth resuscitation to* ANGELA *using the tube instead of touching her mouth.* ANGELA *responds well to the air blown into her lungs. Normal breathing starts to return to her.*

ANGELA: Thanks for that. *(Chiding him.)* It wasn't so bad, was it?
BARRY: Help me, please! *(He is, after all, stung all over now. He gasps for air. Almost screaming:)* I'm going to die! And all I've done with my short life was lose weight!
ANGELA: You're talking like you're already dead!
BARRY: Just think how you were talking after being stung!
ANGELA: You're right.
BARRY: Come on. *(Gasping.)* What's the hold up? *(Gasping more.)* Give me tube-to-mouth or I'll die!
ANGELA: I don't know if I should.
BARRY: Why?
ANGELA: After the way you treated me.
BARRY: *(Protesting.)* But I just... This is no time for grudges! We have a deal.
ANGELA: Maybe I don't feel like keeping up my end of it.
BARRY: I'm sure you're a nice person despite everything you've been through. It's not your nature to be vicious. You only get that way when somebody's been bad to you. I apologize. *(Choking.)* Look, I've SEEN THE LIGHT, haven't I? I'm learning cooperation – the first part. Now it's your turn... *(Pause.)* If I die, you'll have to live for the rest of your life knowing that you killed someone. You don't want that on your conscience, do you? *(Starting to weep.)* If you want me to beg for it, then I'm begging you for it! Do it to me!
ANGELA: Don't beg. It reminds me of some of the movies I was in.

*ANGELA gives BARRY mouth-to-mouth resuscitation without the tube. After receiving the air, BARRY's breathing starts to normalize.*

BARRY: Thanks. Thanks for saving my life.

*Pause.*

ANGELA: I said I'd teach you cooperation. Here's another lesson: I'm NOT a transvestite. I'm a TRANSEXUAL. And that means OFFICIALLY I'm a woman. *(Pause. Feeling sexually attracted to him.)* You know, you're a good-looking guy.

BARRY *groans.*

BARRY: Don't even think of it!

*After his remark BARRY falls back to the ground in exhaustion.*

## About the Playwright

Lance Tait's plays have been produced or received staged readings in New York, Los Angeles, Denver, Toronto, Paris, the United Kingdom, and at the American Repertory Theatre. In 2002, in Paris, Tait founded Theatre Metropole. He writes a variety of works for the stage and is also active as a filmmaker. Other theater books by Lance Tait include: *Three Essential Plays: Car Door Shave*, *Gambling Fever*, *Neither God Nor Master*; *The Black Cat and Other Plays Adapted From Stories by Edgar Allan Poe*; *Synesthesia*; *The Fall of the House of Usher and Other Plays Inspired by Edgar Allan Poe*; *Mad Cow Disease in America*, *Something Special, and Other Plays*; *Edwin Booth*; and *Miss Julie*, *David Mamet Fan Club, and Other Plays*. Websites: www.lancetait.com and www.theatremetropole.org.